TEACHER'S GUIDE

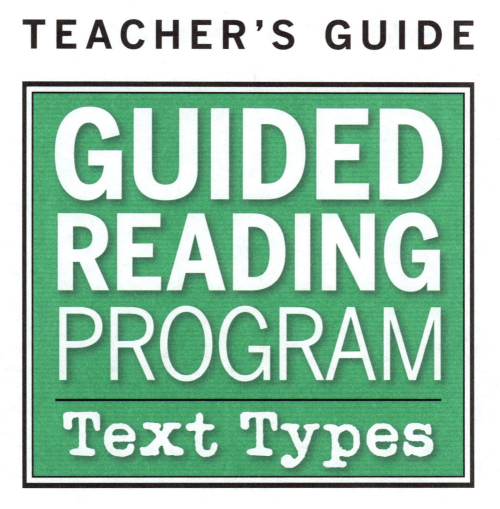

GUIDED READING PROGRAM
Text Types

by Gay Su Pinnell
The Ohio State University

and

Irene Fountas
Lesley University

Book cover credits (p. 154): *The Hunger Games* by Suzanne Collins. Copyright © 2008 by Suzanne Collins. Published by Scholastic Inc. Cover art by Tim O'Brien. *Owen & Mzee: The True Story of a Remarkable Friendship* by Isabella Hatkoff, Craig Hatkoff, and Dr. Paula Kahumbu, photographs by Peter Greste. Photographs copyright © 2006, 2005 by Peter Greste. Published by Scholastic Inc. *Popcorn* by Karen Alexander. Copyright © 2010 by Scholastic Inc. Published by Scholastic Inc. Cover: iStockphoto.com/Yvan Dubé. *The Devil's Arithmetic* by Jane Yolen. Copyright © 1988 by Jane Yolen. Published by Scholastic Inc. by arrangement with Penguin Group (USA) Inc. *Let's Eat!* by Margaret Bellings, illustrated by Amy Lam. Copyright © 2010 by Scholastic Inc. Published by Scholastic Inc. *Little Piglets* by Cynthia Rothman, illustrated by Stevie Mahardhika. Copyright © 2010 by Scholastic Inc. Published by Scholastic Inc. *Sea Animals* by Annie Thomas. Copyright © 2010 by Scholastic Inc. Published by Scholastic Inc. Cover: (l) iStockphoto.com/Kristian Sekulic, (r) Shutterstock/Khoroshunova Olga, (b) Shutterstock. *Bears (Now I Know)* by Melvin and Gilda Berger. Text copyright © 2006 by Melvin and Gilda Berger. Published by Scholastic Inc. Cover: Adam Jones/Photo Researchers, Inc. *The Rain Came Down* by David Shannon. Text and illustrations copyright © 2000 by David Shannon. Published by Scholastic Inc. *Why Mosquitoes Buzz in People's Ears* by Verna Aardema, illustrated by Leo and Diane Dillon. Pictures copyright © 1975 by Leo and Diane Dillon. Published by Scholastic Inc. by arrangement with Penguin Group (USA) Inc. *Crafts* by Betsey Chessen and Pamela Chanko. Copyright © 1999 by Scholastic Inc. Published by Scholastic Inc.

ISBN-13: 978-0-545-32007-8
ISBN-10: 0-545-32007-0

2 3 4 5 6 7 8 9 10   40   19 18 17 16 15 14 13 12 11

Table of Contents

Using the Guided Reading Program

USING YOUR
GUIDED READING PROGRAM

The *Scholastic Guided Reading Program* is a varied collection of books that are categorized by the kind and level of challenge they offer children as they are learning to read. The Guided Reading Program consists of 260 books organized into 26 levels of difficulty—Levels A–Z. Many different characteristics of the texts are considered in determining the level of challenge and support a particular book or shorter story presents.

Advantages of a Leveled Book Collection

A leveled book set has many advantages, including the following:

- It provides experience with a wide variety of texts within a level.
- It makes it easier to select books for groups of children.
- It lends itself to flexible grouping.
- It provides a way to assess children's progress.
- It provides a basic book collection that can be expanded over time.

Multiple Copies of Books	Six copies of each book are provided so that children in small groups will have access to their own copies. Having a collection of books on various levels, with multiple copies of each book, allows you to consider individual strengths when grouping and selecting books. To help you identify a book's level quickly, you may place a Guided Reading Program sticker for the level on the front or back of each book cover.
Flexibility of Use	With a gradient of text, grouping can be more flexible. Children might read only some of the books in a level, and not necessarily in the same sequence. In addition, children may change groups based on individual needs. The **Characteristics of Text** and **Behaviors to Notice and Support** on pages 96–121 will assist you in placing children in the appropriate levels.
	If you note that some students need extra support for a particular text or that the selection is too difficult for most of the group, you can abandon guided reading and instead use shared reading to experience the book. Then you can select an easier book the next day. As students progress, have them reread books on a lower level for enjoyment. Students will become more confident readers as they reread a book for meaning with no need for problem solving.
Adding to the Guided Reading Program	The Guided Reading Program has been designed with adaptability in mind, so you may add copies of children's and your own favorite books to the library. You may place a Guided Reading Program sticker for the suggested level on each book you add.

Variety Within Levels in the Collection

When working with groups in classroom reading, a broad base of text is needed. The Guided Reading Program provides this broad base. Readers who experience only one kind of book may develop a narrow range of strategies for processing text. With a leveled set, difficulty is controlled because all text characteristics have been factored in. Yet the level of text is not artificially controlled because the variety of text characteristics occurs within natural story language.

The early levels of the Guided Reading Program introduce students to reading print. While reading at these beginning levels, students apply phonics skills, develop a core of high-frequency words, work with print in a variety of layouts, and engage with a variety of high-interest texts.

Books at later levels (Levels J and beyond) include a wider range of text. Within each level, literary texts are included. Essentially, there are three kinds of books at these levels, although there is variety within each category.

- **First, there are picture books at a more sophisticated level than before. These picture books provide an opportunity to expand vocabulary, to interpret stories, and to recognize how illustrations contribute to the story. Like the short story, picture books provide the advanced reader with complex reading material that does not take several days to complete.**

- **Second, there are informational books that are generally shorter. These present complex ideas and some technical language. They challenge students to acquire and discuss ideas and information and to go beyond the text to research topics of interest to them.**

- **Third, there are longer stories and chapter books. These longer selections provide an opportunity for readers to sustain reading over time, remembering details and getting to know characters as they develop.**

FACTORS CONSIDERED IN
LEVELING BOOKS

In placing a book, short story, or article along a gradient of text, multiple characteristics of text are considered. Here is a sample list.

Book and Print Features
Refers to the physical aspects of the text—what readers cope with in terms of length, size, print layout, and font size. It also refers to the interpretation of illustrations and the relationships between information in graphics and the body of the text.

- How many words are in the book?
- How many lines of text are on each page?
- How many pages are in the book?
- What size is the print?
- How much space is there between words and lines?
- How easy is it to find information?
- What is the relationship between print and illustrations?
- Are there graphics (photos, diagrams, maps) that provide essential information and how easy are the graphics to interpret?
- What are the features of print layout? (For example, do sentences begin on the left or do they "wrap around" so that end punctuation must be relied upon?)
- Is print placed in standard, predictable places on the pages or is it used in creative ways that require the reader's flexibility?
- Do the size and shape of book, binding, and layout play a role in text interpretation?

Genre
Means the "type" or "kind" and refers to a classification system formed to provide a way of talking about what texts are like (fiction—including realistic fiction, fantasy, traditional literature; and nonfiction—including biography, autobiography, and informational texts).

- What is the "genre" or "kind" of book?
- What special demands does this genre make on readers?
- Is this an easy or more difficult example of the genre?

Content
Refers to the subject matter that readers are required to understand as they read both fiction and nonfiction texts.

- What background information is essential for understanding this text?
- What new information will readers need to grasp to read the text?
- How accessible is the content to the readers?

Themes and Ideas
Refers to the "big picture," the universality of the problem in the text and its relevance to people's lives.

- What is the theme of the text?
- Are there multiple themes that the reader must understand and be able to talk about?
- How accessible are the "big ideas" to the reader?

Language and Literary Features

Refers to the writer's style and use of literary devices. Literary features are those elements typically used in literature to capture imagination, stir emotions, create empathy or suspense, give readers a sense that the characters and story are real, and make readers care about the outcome of the plot. Nonfiction books may incorporate some literary features.

- From what perspective is the story or informational text written?
- Does the book include devices such as headings, labels, and captions?
- Are graphical elements such as diagrams, tables, charts, and maps included?
- To what degree does the writer use literary language, such as metaphor?
- How easy is it to understand the characters and their motivations and development?
- Is character development essential to the story?
- Is dialogue assigned (using he said) or unassigned with longer stretches of interchange that the reader must follow and attribute to one character or another?
- How are characters revealed through what they say or think and what others say or think about them?
- How essential to the story are understandings about setting and plot?

Vocabulary and Words

Refers to the words and their accessibility to readers. Vocabulary generally refers to the meaning of words that readers may decode but not understand. Word solving refers to both decoding and to understanding meaning.

- What is the frequency of multisyllabic words in the text?
- How complex are word meanings? (For example, are readers required to understand multiple meanings or subtle shades of meaning of words?)
- What prior knowledge is needed to understand the vocabulary of the text?
- How many content or technical words are included in the text? How complex are these words?
- Does informational text utilize timeless verb constructions? (Ants carry sand as opposed to carried.)
- Are generic noun constructions used in informational and/or nonfiction text?

Sentence Complexity

Refers to the syntactic patterns readers will encounter in the text; sentences may be simple (short, with one subject and predicate) or complex (longer, with embedded clauses).

- What is the average length of sentences in the text?
- To what degree do sentences contain embedded clauses?
- What is the sentence style of the writer?
- Are there complex sentences joined by and, but, or other conjunctions?
- Are paragraphs organized so that readers can recognize lead sentences and main ideas?

Punctuation

Refers to the graphic symbols that signal the way text should be read to reflect the author's meaning.

- What punctuation symbols are used in the text?
- What do readers need to notice about punctuation in order to fully understand the text?
- What punctuation is essential for readers to notice to read with fluency and phrasing?

Using Leveled Books With Readers

The success of guided reading depends on many factors other than text characteristics. These, of course, have to do with the young readers using the texts as well as teacher-student interactions and include:

- The reader's prior knowledge of the topic, including vocabulary and concepts.
- The reader's prior experience with texts that have similar features.
- The way the teacher introduces the text.
- The supportive interactions between the teacher and students before, during, and after reading.
- The level of interest teachers help students build.

Level-by-Level Descriptions

Characteristics of text for each level in the Guided Reading Program are listed on pages 96–121. These descriptions are general: not every book included in a level will have every characteristic noted. Also listed are some important behaviors to notice and support at each level. As you use these books with students, you will notice how they support and challenge readers.

Other Resources

You may want to refer to the following resources for descriptions of guided reading as well as additional books for each level:

- **Duke, Nell K., and Bennett-Armistead, V. Susan, 2003.** *Reading & Writing Informational Text in the Primary Grades.* **New York, NY: Scholastic Inc.**
- **Fountas, I. C., and Pinnell, G. S., 2008.** *Benchmark Assessment System 1 and 2.* **Portsmouth, NH: Heinemann.**
- **Fountas, I. C., and Pinnell, G. S., 1996.** *Guided Reading: Good First Teaching for All Children.* **Portsmouth, NH: Heinemann.**
- **Fountas, I. C., and Pinnell, G. S., 2001.** *Guiding Readers and Writers, Grades 3–6: Teaching Comprehension, Genre, and Content Literacy.* **Portsmouth, NH: Heinemann.**
- **Fountas, I. C., and Pinnell, G. S., 2005.** *Leveled Books, K–8: Matching Texts to Readers for Effective Teaching.* **Portsmouth, NH: Heinemann.**
- **Fountas, I. C., and Pinnell, G. S., 1999.** *Voices on Word Matters.* **Portsmouth, NH: Heinemann.**
- **Pinnell, G. S., and Fountas, I. C., 2007.** *The Continuum of Literacy Learning, Grades K–8: Behaviors and Understandings to Notice, Teach, and Support.* **Portsmouth, NH: Heinemann.**
- **Pinnell, G. S., and Fountas, I. C., 1998.** *Word Matters: Teaching Phonics and Spelling in the Reading/Writing Classroom.* **Portsmouth, NH: Heinemann.**
- **Fountas, I. C., and Pinnell, G. S., 2006.** *Teaching for Comprehending and Fluency: Thinking, Talking, and Writing About Reading, K–8.* **Portsmouth, NH: Heinemann.**

WHAT IS
GUIDED READING?

Guided reading is an instructional approach that involves a teacher working with a small group of students who demonstrate similar reading behaviors and can all read similar levels of texts. The text is easy enough for students to read with your skillful support. The text offers challenges and opportunities for problem solving, but is easy enough for students to read with some fluency. You choose selections that help students expand their strategies.

What is the purpose of guided reading?

You select books that students can read with about 90 percent accuracy. Students can understand and enjoy the story because it's accessible to them through their own strategies, supported by your introduction. They focus on meaning but use problem-solving strategies to figure out words they don't know, deal with difficult sentence structure, and understand concepts or ideas they have never before encountered in print.

Why is guided reading important?

Guided reading gives students the chance to apply the strategies they already know to new text. You provide support, but the ultimate goal is independent reading.

When are children ready for guided reading?

Developing readers have already gained important understandings about how print works. These students know how to monitor their own reading. They have the ability to check on themselves or search for possibilities and alternatives if they encounter a problem when reading. For these readers, the guided reading experience is a powerful way to support the development of reading strategies.

The ultimate goal of guided reading is reading a variety of texts with ease and deep understanding. Silent reading means rapid processing of texts with most attention on meaning, which is achieved as readers move past beginning levels (H, I, J). At all levels, students read orally with fluency and phrasing.

Matching Books to Readers

The teacher selects a text for a small group of students who are similar in their reading behaviors at a particular point in time. In general, the text is about right for students in the group. It is not too easy, yet not too hard, and offers a variety of challenges to help readers become flexible problem solvers. You should choose Guided Reading Program books for students that:

- match their knowledge base.
- help them take the next step in learning to read.
- are interesting to them.
- offer just enough challenge to support problem solving while still supporting fluency and meaning.

Supporting Students' Reading

In working with students in guided reading, you constantly balance the difficulty of the text with support for students reading the text. You introduce the story to the group, support individuals through brief interactions while they read, and guide them to talk together afterwards about the words and ideas in the text. In this way, you refine text selection and help individual readers move forward in developing a reading process.

Good readers employ a wide range of word-solving strategies, including analysis of sound-letter relationships and word parts. They must figure out words that are embedded in different kinds of texts. Reading a variety of books enables them to go beyond reading individual words to interpreting language and its subtle meanings.

For more specific teaching suggestions, see individual cards for each book title.

Procedure for Guided Reading

- The teacher works with a small group of students with similar needs.
- The teacher provides introductions to the text that support students' later attempts at problem solving.
- Each student reads the whole text or a unified part of the text.
- Readers figure out new words while reading for meaning.
- The teacher prompts, encourages, and confirms students' attempts at problem solving.
- The teacher and student engage in meaningful conversations about what they are reading.
- The teacher and student revisit the text to demonstrate and use a range of comprehension strategies.

ORGANIZING YOUR CLASSROOM FOR GUIDED READING

adapted from *Guided Reading: Making It Work* (Schulman and Payne, 2000)

Good management begins with a thoughtful room arrangement and careful selection of materials; the way you organize furniture and supplies will support the learning that takes place within your classroom. For guided reading to be effective, the rest of the class must be engaged in other literacy activities that do not require direct teacher involvement. For most classes, this means literacy centers that accommodate small groups of students. So, a strategically arranged classroom for guided reading would have a class library, inviting spots for individual work, spaces for whole-class gatherings and small-group meetings, and several literacy centers.

Arranging the room and organizing materials for effective reading and writing workshops takes thought and planning. So before the school year even begins, consider the activities you're planning for your class and the physical layout of your room. With a little ingenuity, you can provide an environment that will support learning all year long.

Scheduling for Guided Reading

To determine the time you'll need for guided reading, consider the number of students in your class and the range of reading abilities they possess. Then create your initial groupings; the ideal group size is four to six, though guided reading groups might range from three to eight. Place below-grade or struggling readers in smaller groups. Keep in mind that sessions are short—often 10–15 minutes for emergent readers, and 15–30 minutes for more advanced readers. You will want to meet with at-risk groups every day; five meetings over a two-week period for more advanced groups are typical. You'll also want to allow yourself some time for assessment—taking a running record, jotting anecdotal notes, or conducting oral interviews, for example. Finally, allow a few minutes between groups to check in with the rest of the class.

THE SCHOLASTIC
GUIDED READING CLASSROOM

Scholastic Guided Reading Programs support a comprehensive reading program by integrating guided instruction, assessment, and independent practice into your classroom. Here's what the Guided Reading classroom looks like:

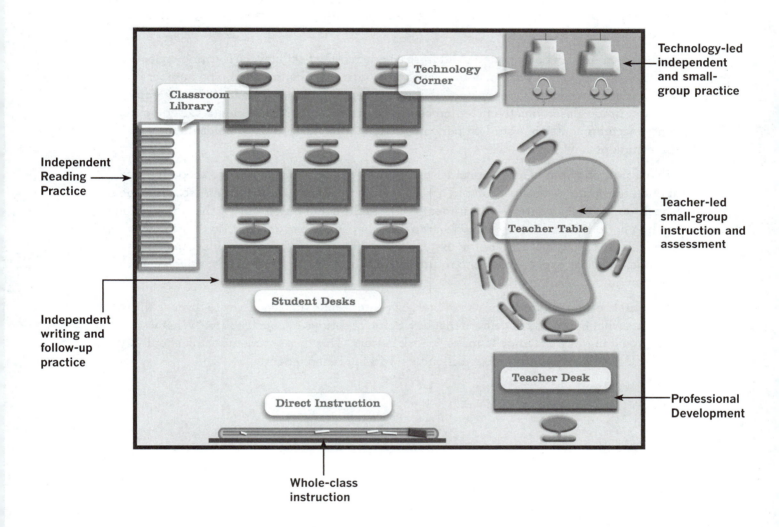

Technology Corner

Classroom Library

Technology-led independent and small-group practice

Independent Reading Practice

Teacher Table

Teacher-led small-group instruction and assessment

Student Desks

Independent writing and follow-up practice

Teacher Desk

Direct Instruction

Professional Development

Whole-class instruction

SETTING UP
LITERACY CENTERS

adapted from *Guided Reading: Making It Work* (Schulman and Payne, 2000)

As a way of managing the time to meet with small groups of students, teachers often use literacy centers. At literacy centers, students continue to participate in purposeful and authentic literacy activities. These centers provide many opportunities to practice the skills real readers and writers use. They take the place of traditional worksheets and are not meant to be graded.

Literacy centers can be designed to address a wide range of skill levels, learning styles, and interests. Students work in heterogeneous groups that change often. The number of students at each center depends upon the type of center and the space for it. For example, in one first-grade classroom, the listening center has stations for four students, the computer center accommodates one student per computer, and the library center holds up to three students.

When arranging your centers, consider the number of students you want to accommodate at once, the space you have available, and the topics that you want to cover. Also think about transitions between centers—will students work at the same center during the whole guided reading period? If so, do they know what to do if they finish early? If not, do they know how to move to another center or activity without disturbing you or other class members? Establishing clear expectations and routines will help centers run smoothly, so you can focus on guided reading groups.

When first setting up students' use of literacy centers, take time each day to discuss with students what happened at centers that day. Some questions to consider are, "What went well? What might we change to make it work better?" This helps students think about ways to problem-solve when they meet difficulties working independently.

Things to Consider When Setting Up Literacy Centers

- Establish a manageable number of centers that can be changed easily and routinely.
- Plan time to introduce and demonstrate how each center operates. Some teachers do this during scheduled shared reading/writing time.
- Consider the physical arrangement of the centers to permit movement and a balance of quiet and noisy areas.
- Design centers to meet the range of all learners, addressing a variety of interests and learning styles.
- Have supplies accessible and labeled for independent student use.
- Create signs or charts that communicate functional information and directions, such as "How to Use the CD Player."
- Develop a plan for the rotation of students through centers and a way to keep track of centers.
- Provide an opportunity for students to select centers.
- Develop a signal or a problem-solving technique for students to use while they are at centers and you are working with other students.
- Periodically review what's working and not working at centers.

Managing and Organizing Literacy Centers

There are a variety of ways to organize and manage centers. Some teachers have students select literacy centers, while others choose the centers for the students to ensure they regularly rotate through them. No matter which approach you take, it is important to have a record-keeping system in place to monitor student participation in various centers.

Alternatives to Centers

Instead of centers, some teachers prefer to involve students in productive reading and writing work at their tables or desks. For Kindergarten and Grade 1, remember that children will need a chance to stretch and move periodically.

For students in Grades 3 and above, you will want to phase out most work at centers. For independent work, students can:

- Read silently a book of their choice at their independent level
- Write or draw in response to reading
- Engage in longer projects that involve research, reading, and writing.

GROUPING STUDENTS

Your job is to take each student from his or her present level to a more advanced one. Therefore, there must be assessment of individual students. With class sizes ranging from 20 to 35, grouping for instruction makes sense. As teachers, we want to make learning manageable, while avoiding any negative aspects of grouping.

Fundamentals of Grouping

Assessment of Students' Knowledge Base

Students' knowledge base is the key element in selecting texts and planning instruction for groups so that they can read with 90 percent accuracy and use the skills that assure understanding. Other aspects to consider when selecting the best level for a group include:

- how well developing readers can control a strategy, such as analyzing a new word.
- the kinds of language students find understandable and which they find challenging.
- what concepts they know or what concepts they don't understand.
- the kinds of texts and genres they have experienced. For example, if they have handled only narrative texts, then informational texts may be difficult.

See pages 96–121 for help in assessing which level is best for a group.

Dynamic Grouping

Because students' individual needs change so often, ongoing observation of behavior and assessment of their knowledge and experience are essential to the guided reading process. Students progress at different rates, so regrouping is also ongoing. By grouping in different ways for different purposes, you can avoid labeling students with group names that are symbols of a static achievement level.

As you informally assess students' reading on a daily basis, you may wish to use the descriptions of **Behaviors to Notice and Support** on pages 96–121 for the level of book you are using. A quick, informal observation of students' reading will help you determine if the book was at the appropriate level.

- **Was this book too hard for this student?** If the student can't read it independently with 85–95 percent accuracy and isn't using strategies as he or she reads, then the book is too hard.
- If the student reads with such fluency that there is no need for problem-solving behaviors, then the student should be reading a higher-level text for guided reading. Of course, the lower-level text will be useful for fluency practice.

RUNNING
GUIDED READING GROUPS

Step 1   Select a Book

With students' needs in mind, select a book for a group of two to six. Use the **Characteristics of Text** to determine general level appropriateness and the description of **Behaviors to Notice and Support** to determine if students' reading ability matches that level. (See pages 96–121.)

Depending on available time, each group of readers at Levels A–J might read fewer books but must sustain attention and memory over several days or a week of reading. For readers in Grades 3–6, the goal of independent and guided reading instruction is to enable students to read one chapter book a week or several shorter selections. No two groups will read exactly the same sequence of books, and groups will change as the assessment system helps track progress.

Step 2   Introduce the Book

Introducing the story is probably the most important and most difficult part of guided reading, and it is your opportunity to provide most of the support to the reader. A brief introduction helps a group to read successfully with minimal teacher support. You may tailor the introduction based on the group and the particular text. Depending on the level of difficulty and students' reading abilities, the introduction includes any combination of these elements:

- **a short conversation about the main idea of the text.**
- **a briefing on the author's purpose for writing and some important features of the plot or informational text.**
- **a description of the main characters, facts, or ideas in the book.**
- **a presentation of any unusual or unique language, such as a repetitive refrain or content words.**
- **a discussion of the concepts needed for an understanding of the text by activating prior knowledge.**
- **drawing attention to any aspects of print that you consider important such as captions, headings, charts, and/or tables.**
- **instructions on how much to read and what to do when finished.**

Without actually reading the text to students, frame it in a meaningful way. Using oral language in a way that familiarizes students with some words they will meet in print helps prepare them to read. It isn't necessary to introduce every page, preteach words, or give a purpose for reading. The idea is to help students to be able to move through the text on their own. Any brief intervention should not interfere with the momentum of independent reading.

Step 3 Read the Book

Once the book has been introduced, students are ready to read. Unlike round-robin reading, in which each student reads a page or sentence, each student using guided reading reads the entire text.

- **Each student reads independently and problem-solves on his or her own.**
- **Reading may be oral or silent, depending on level and skill.**

As students read, you are nearby to observe them, providing support when necessary. As they read, note reading behaviors and offer praise when students use a strategy successfully. Students reading in Levels A through J will be reading in a soft whisper. More advanced students will be reading silently. You can sample their oral reading by asking them to lift their voices to an audible level for a page or two. All students continue reading silently at their own rates as you sample oral reading from several of them.

If students have been placed in the appropriate level, they will problem-solve independently. However, if the whole group seems stuck, you may want to stop the group to assist in problem solving. You might also make teaching points, such as pointing out inflectional endings or consonant digraphs. Detours should be brief, not interrupting the momentum of students' reading.

Try to choose one student in the group daily to observe and interact with, helping him or her develop reading strategies, and encouraging the independent use of those strategies.

Step 4 Respond to the Book and Learn About Reading

After students read, first invite them to discuss the meaning of the text. Then select one or two teaching points to bring to their attention. What you select to teach depends on students' needs. You might focus on the meaning of a portion of text, on character interpretation, on information or facts, or on some aspect of word solving, such as multisyllabic words. For example, you might:

- **promote fluency and phrasing by asking students to read aloud a favorite part of the story.**
- **help students focus on key ideas and language by having them find a turning point in the story, an informational part, or a description.**
- **help students figure out new, longer words by having them focus on word parts or known words.**
- **engage students in actively exploring how words work—building words, changing words, and noticing their features.**
- **help students interpret information provided in nonfiction features such as maps, charts, graphs, etc.**

By following up the reading of a text in this way, you are helping students develop strategies that they can apply to the reading of other books. You are helping them learn the "how to" of reading and to move forward toward the goal of developing a reading process.

Step 5 Assess Behavior

The day after a new text is read, record the ability level of one child and note any progress. The **Behaviors to Notice and Support** can help you assess.

GUIDED READING AND THE
STRUGGLING READER

Guided reading groups shift as students' reading abilities and interests change. As you work with your guided reading groups, you will be able to identify students who need extra help. Guided reading provides many advantages in helping these students. After assessing their reading levels and pinpointing what skills and strategies they need help with, you can move struggling readers to groups that provide support. Within these groups, struggling readers will be able to read more with greater accuracy and fluency, as they will be working with text at their level. You will also be able to work with them on word skills that other students may already know.

Select books that match your students' reading levels.

Any group of struggling readers will likely vary widely in their abilities. Because of this, you will need to be careful in selecting texts that are interesting, yet not too difficult. Struggling readers are usually slow readers because they have been trying to read texts that are too challenging. Slow reading interferes with comprehension, but with appropriate texts, students will be able to increase their speed and improve their comprehension. Gradually, students should be able to take on more challenging texts as their reading abilities and confidence improve.

Involve students in reading every day.

Struggling readers need to spend more time actually reading than doing activities related to reading. Plan daily guided reading time for these students to increase the amount of time they read with support.

Plan additional time to introduce and discuss texts.

Extra time may be needed for introductions and discussions before and after reading to guide students in anticipating what they will read and then thinking about and understanding the text. This extra time will help students learn how to approach text as they prepare to read. It will also give them opportunities to discuss what they have learned and to hear others' ideas. Encourage students to ask questions, and teach them how to find answers in the text.

Include working with words in guided reading lessons.

At the end of each guided reading lesson, spend a few minutes showing students the principles of how words work. Have them apply the principles to selected examples. To make this work more interesting, create word games.

Allow time for silent reading.

As students' reading abilities improve, give them time to read silently as well as orally. Silent reading is beneficial in that it is faster than oral reading and text is easier to comprehend.

USING **RESPONSE TO INTERVENTION** IN THE GUIDED READING CLASSROOM

One tool educators can use to identify and help struggling readers is the Response to Intervention Framework. Response to Intervention (RTI) originated in 2002 with the Individuals with Disabilities Education Act (IDEA). Prior to 2004, children were identified with a specific learning disability through documentation of a mismatch between a child's IQ and academic achievement. In years past, this typically led to a special education placement. The new law requires states to identify children based on their responses to research-based intervention, the theory being that their response to good instruction is a more reliable process for identifying learning disabilities.

While its premise was simple, its results are revolutionary: students who struggle with reading no longer face a battery of diagnostic tests administered by a school psychologist which, in years past, typically led to a special education placement. Now classroom teachers use a series of systematic assessments of their choice (or the choice of their district) to determine students' strengths and weaknesses. With that data in hand, they immediately create a thoughtful program of systematic, sensitive support for these students and intervene with targeted small-group instruction, typically framed around three tiers that represent a "continuum of supports" (National Center on Response to Intervention, 2010, p. 4). The advantage of using RTI is that students who are at risk of having reading difficulties are identified early. Early identification can prevent some students from being placed in special education when all they need is a short period of intense intervention. Further, student progress is carefully monitored.

In practice, RTI can look very different from school to school, as it is tailored to fit specific situations and students. However, RTI programs do have common elements:

- **Instruction is based on individual students' needs.**
- **The program is preventative and proactive.**
- **All students are assessed.**
- **Assessments used must be reliable and valid.**
- **At-risk students are provided with various levels of intense intervention.**
- **Student progress is closely monitored.**
- **Professional development is a critical part of the program.**
- **Strong administrative support ensures commitment and resources.**

In the typical 3-tier model, Tier 1 is intended to represent high-quality core classroom instruction for all children. Tier 2 gives children who are not showing adequate progress more support, often through small-group or one-on-one instruction and more frequent progress monitoring so that instruction can be tailored to each student's needs. Tier 3 instruction is typically an intensive, often one-on-one intervention conducted by a specialized teacher.

Matching Great Text to Readers

In any RTI classroom, once students have been assessed and their challenges understood, the next step is selecting texts that students can read. As Richard Allington noted, "Whenever we design an intervention for struggling readers, the single most critical factor that will determine the success of the effort is matching struggling readers with texts they can actually read with a high level of accuracy, fluency, and comprehension" (2009). The principles underlying guided reading remind us that readers need text that they can read across a range of genres that showcase a variety of text types. In this way, students will learn how to make critical reading adjustments to accommodate different kinds of texts. (See *Guided Reading: Text Types*, pp. 32–35: "The Importance of Reading a Variety of Texts and Genres.")

Tier 1

Tier I, or primary intervention, centers on core reading instruction—informed by the best available information on how to teach reading. To that end, research (Biancarosa, Bryk, & Dexter, 2009; Johnston, 2010) demonstrates that guided reading provides a setting within which the explicit teaching of strategic processing behaviors—word solving, comprehending, and reading with fluency—is ideal. Indeed, CIERA (Center for the Improvement of Early Reading Achievement) investigated the practices of accomplished classroom teachers who were helping strugglers beat the odds and achieve. What they found is noteworthy: "Time spent in small-group instruction for reading distinguished the most effective schools from the other schools in the study" (Taylor, 2000). Tier 1 intervention is accomplished through the use of high-quality reading materials and carefully selected leveled texts that meet the needs of all students. Guided reading instruction aligns perfectly with the goals and targeted support of Tier I intervention:

1. **Introduce text to students, providing background information and pointing out such text features as structure, topics, vocabulary, plot, illustrations, and other graphics.**

2. **Intervene as needed to demonstrate specific comprehension strategies as well as prompt and reinforce students' thinking.**

3. **Reinforce effective problem solving of words using the meaning, language, and print.**

4. **Demonstrate, reinforce, or prompt self-correcting errors that interfere with meaning making.**

5. **Demonstrate, reinforce, or prompt using punctuation to aid meaning, reading with phrasing, pausing appropriately, stressing the correct words, or using expression.**

6. **Guide a discussion—after students have read—that probes for deeper meaning and helps to extend their thinking.**

7. **Link to writing as yet another way to extend thinking.**

The majority of readers, both on-level and vulnerable, will thrive and succeed with Tier I intervention. Allington notes (2009) that this potent mix of informed, strategic reading instruction in a small-group setting coupled with engaging text that students can read is the key to success for most struggling readers.

Tier 2

On the other hand, if students fail to respond successfully to Tier 1 intervention, the next step is to increase and intensify the intervention. Working within small groups—and providing explicit, scaffolded, targeted intervention that continues to demonstrate, prompt for, and reinforce problem-solving strategies—in addition to daily core instruction is key. Again, guided reading (Fountas and Pinnell, 2006) provides an ideal instructional setting for this intensive teaching; guided reading supports and encourages teachers to:

1. draw attention to the ways in which words work, for example, pointing out first letters, plurals, word endings, consonant clusters, vowel pairs, syllables, and the like.

2. watch for opportunities as students read to teach, prompt, and demonstrate how to take words apart; teach word solving rapidly and efficiently.

3. engage students in word work and help them attend to meaningful word parts and meanings such as affixes, base words, root words, homophones, synonyms, and antonyms.

4. help students develop the automatic word recognition and comprehending strategies that enable fluent reading.

5. demonstrate, prompt for, and reinforce all the strategies that accelerate proficient reading—comprehending, phonics, and fluency.

Tier 3

Occasionally, despite best efforts through your Tier 1/core reading instruction and the intensified intervention of Tier 2, a few at-risk strugglers may need even more extensive intervention. Within Tier 3, intense, extensive guided reading support coupled with a wide range of texts students can read is still a best bet for moving kids into successful, proficient reading. Teachers may work one-on-one with students and engage the services of a literacy specialist or, as needed, they may consider referring at-risk students for special education testing and services.

In this way, RTI coupled with guided reading accomplishes two goals: it 1) develops a more valid way of identifying students who are struggling as readers; and 2) catches students at risk of failure through early intervention. At the same time, RTI elevates teachers' professional understanding of effective reading instruction and improves the overall approach to helping students who don't initially "get" reading. Ultimately, RTI moves us away from a model of failure to one of prevention.

Guided Reading: The Ideal Core Support for RTI

As Gay Su Pinnell and Irene Fountas outline in their comprehensive *When Readers Struggle: Teaching That Works,* when it comes to supporting striving readers, there are "three keys to success": 1) expert teaching; 2) excellent reading material expertly matched to each reader; 3) strong instruction design (2009).

Guided reading is a highly effective form of small-group instruction. Based on assessment data, teachers bring together a group of readers who are similar enough in their reading development that they can be taught together. They read independently at about the same level and can take on a new text that is just a little more challenging. Teachers support the reading in a way that enables students to read more challenging texts with effective processing— and, in this way, expand their reading powers. And it's this exemplary core instruction, continually informed by the teaching-assessing loop, that forms the heart of Response to Intervention.

GUIDED READING AND
21st CENTURY LEARNING SKILLS

For our guide to 21st century learning skills, we turn first to Bernie Trilling and Charles Fadel's definitive book on the matter, *21st Century Learning Skills: Learning for Life in Our Times* (2009). The authors address the skills in three categories (p. xxvi):

Learning and Innovation Skills

Critical thinking and problem solving

Communication and collaboration

Creativity and innovation

Digital Literacy Skills

Information literacy

Media literacy

Information and Communication Technologies (ICT) literacy

Career and Life Skills

Flexibility and adaptability

Initiative and self-direction

Social and cross-cultural interaction

Productivity and accountability

Leadership and responsibilities

The Mile Guide: Milestones for Improving Learning & Education, assembled by The Partnership for 21st Century Skills, the leading advocacy organization focused on infusing 21st century skills into education, outlines six new literacies our students will need for future success:

1. Civic Literacy
2. Technology Literacy
3. Global Literacy
4. Economic Literacy
5. Health Literacy
6. Environmental Literacy

Stanford University scholar Linda Darling-Hammond sums up 21st century learning this way: "The new mission of schools is to prepare students to work at jobs that do not yet exist, creating ideas and solutions for products and problems that have not been identified, using technologies that have not yet been invented" (2010, p. 2).

Guided Reading Makes It All Possible

If we consider Trilling and Fadel's lists of 21st century learning skills, *critical thinking* and *problem solving* seem to encapsulate what is needed to live successfully in our increasingly complex world, together with collaboration, communication, innovation, flexibility, and initiative. It is not surprising to learn that these key 21st century literate capacities can originate with the strategic processing skills children acquire through their rich immersion in engaging texts coupled with the exemplary instruction realized through guided reading.

The "anemic teaching" (Darling-Hammond, 2010) of the last two decades—rote memorization and low level test-driven thinking—must give way to robust learning and habits of mind. AFT secretary-treasurer Antonia Cortese and education critic Diane Ravitch capture what's needed:

> We believe in the importance of preparing students to live and succeed in a global economy. We don't think that the mastery of basic skills is sufficient for this goal. What we need is an education system that teaches deep knowledge, that values creativity and originality, and that values thinking skills.

The days of memorizing isolated facts are gone. Guided reading provides the instructional context and cognitive processing that is applicable to all text, including digital, hypertexted, and social-media generated, and makes the charge of 21st century learning possible. Further, the small-group setting and robust discussion of guided reading foster the kinds of collaboration that Trilling recommends. Inside guided reading groups, students work together to think critically, make connections, draw conclusions, and discuss, write about, and act on their new understandings. These are the skills they learn from reading a wide range of text, interacting with multiple genres, and, within the framework of guided reading, thinking within, beyond, and about the text they encounter.

These days, students are facing new challenges on an unprecedented scale. They need books and access to the critical thinking they offer. As new media literacies such as wikis, blogs, and online social networks burst onto the scene, knowing how to read critically and evaluate the worth of the "text" are essential. To that end, the provocative discussions that books in the Guided Reading Program evoke can provide invaluable training.

Students are reading, writing, and sharing what they read and write through a vast network of social media. In the 21st century, *skilled, passionate, habitual, critical readers* (Atwell, 2008), aided by caring, professionally informed teachers (Fountas and Pinnell, 2010), will read their way to academic success and, beyond school, into productive lives rich with the promise that reading makes possible.

GUIDED READING AND
COMMON CORE STATE STANDARDS

The Common Core State Standards, spearheaded by the Council of Chief State School Officers (CCSSO) and the National Governors Association (NGA), are a response to the call by the states to "create the next generation of K–12 standards in order to help ensure that all students are college and career ready in literacy no later than the end of high school" (p. 3). The Common Core State Standards (CCSS) build on research and international models and draw information and inspiration from numerous sources, including state departments of education, professional organizations, scholars, educators from kindergarten through college, parents, and concerned citizens. As a result, the Standards are:

1. **research and evidence-based.**
2. **aligned with college and work expectations.**
3. **rigorous.**
4. **internationally benchmarked.**

Matched Goals: CCSS and Guided Reading Instruction

The Common Core State Standards call for reading across a wide range of increasingly complex texts. And, in perfect alignment with the CCSS, guided reading teachers strive to help students read and comprehend increasingly complex literary and informational texts independently and proficiently.

The research that supports guided reading informs the Common Core State Standards (CCSS) as well, just as matching texts to readers and systematically increasing text complexity, a basic tenet of CCSS, lie at the core of guided reading. It is no surprise, then, that the description of guided reading, provided by Braunger and Lewis (2008), reflects the instructional call to action touted by CCSS:

> Guided reading gives students the opportunity to read a wide variety of texts; to problem solve while reading for meaning; to use strategies on complete, extended text; and to attend to words in texts. Guided reading requires that a teacher's selection of text, guidance, demonstration, and explanation be made explicit to the reader (p. 78; cited in Kucer, 2008).

What It Means to Be a Literate Person in the 21st Century

The Common Core State Standards define literacy for 21st century students as the ability to *apply* what they know to new life challenges. And this seems wise, as information is exploding exponentially. Indeed, the amount of new technical information is doubling every 72 hours (Darling-Hammond, 2010). Given the astronomical number of facts the digital universe represents, helping our students learn how to use their minds, read critically, and get at the heart of what they need to address must become our instructional focus.

To this end, the Standards call for a special emphasis on informational text and, in a similar vein, the 2009 reading framework of the National Assessment of Educational Progress (NAEP) systematically increases the proportion of informational text on its assessment as students advance through the grades.

This chart represents the distribution of literary and information passages by grade in the 2009 NAEP Reading Framework across all content areas.

Grade	Literary	Informational
4	50%	50%
8	45%	55%
12	30%	70%

Developing "Literate Capacities"

The Common Core State Standards aim to create students who advance through the grades developing as fully literate. In the overview of the CCSS (2010), a student who has mastered the standards in reading, writing, speaking, listening, and language is able to "exhibit with increasing fullness and regularity" seven "capacities of the literate individual," or what might also be regarded as seven essential habits of mind. Teachers who adopt the strategic, exemplary instructional practices of guided reading find it serves as a superhighway to creating confident learners who can read critically, ask essential questions, follow a line of inquiry, articulate their own ideas, and in general, enjoy the life of the mind that robust literacy makes possible. As outlined by the Common Core State Standards (and achievable through guided reading), students develop these literate capacities.

Demonstrate independence	Students are able to comprehend and critique a wide range of text types and genres, pinpoint the key message, request clarification, and ask relevant questions. As students engage in lively, content-rich discussions, their vocabularies grow, as does their control over Standard English, and their ability to build on others' ideas while articulating their own. Ultimately, students become self-directed learners, obtaining support from teachers, peers, authorities, and other resources—print, digital, and multimedia—that they need for their own learning.
Build strong content knowledge	Students engage with rich content through wide-ranging texts of quality; in the process, they learn to read purposefully, often led by their own essential questions. They hone their general knowledge while they gain content-specific information, all of which they learn to share with others through writing and speaking.
Respond to varying demands of audience	Students become text- and audience-sensitive, understanding that different texts arrive in different formats and serve different purposes (consider the audience of a recipe versus a poem or the delivery of an advertising jingle versus a persuasive essay). As students are immersed in multiple examples of text types, exploring their form and function, they soon learn to control the various texts themselves, adjusting their purpose for reading, writing, and speaking in ways that align with the task at hand.

Comprehend as well as critique	In this era of print and multimedia bombardment, teachers recognize that their ultimate aim is to help their students become critical readers, so they not only understand the message but also can question its assumptions, relevance, and validity. Learning how to be thoughtfully discerning is a key skill in 21st century learning.
Value evidence	Again, with the explosion of new information, students need to learn how to back up what they say and write with evidence. The ability to articulate what they believe and why—citing relevant evidence to make key points—and expecting the same of others is, today, a standard skill and expectation.
Use technology and digital media strategically and capably	Technology offers a universe of learning, but students need guidance in how to conduct efficient, productive online searches and then integrate what they learn into other media. And, students also need to have a sense of what technology can and cannot do—what are its limitations? And what technical tool is the best fit for each task?
Come to understand other perspectives and cultures	Reading in general and literature in particular have always offered the promise of opportunities to experience other lives, universes, and emotional fields. A kaleidoscope of culture, language, human values, opinions, and perspectives flashes into focus through reading, and helps to shape the awareness, sensitivity, and appreciation of a literate person.

How Guided Reading Helps Students Develop the "Literate Capacities" Promoted by the CCSS

Literate capacities begin with understanding. In order to crack open and comprehend a text, our students need to engage in three kinds of thinking:

- **Thinking Within the Text**
- **Thinking Beyond the Text**
- **Thinking About the Text**

These mental acts of processing happen simultaneously and, largely, unconsciously. Fountas and Pinnell explain that our goal, as teachers, is to "enable readers to assimilate, apply, and coordinate systems of strategic actions without being fully aware that they are doing so" (p. 45). (For a more complete explanation of these processing actions, see *Guided Reading: Text Types*, pp. 42–45.) But it is engagement with text within the context of guided reading which enables the habits of mind or literate capacities promoted by the CCSS.

To understand more completely how the strategic actions students develop through guided reading build the literate capacities the CCSS promote, let's look at the overlap between the College and Career Readiness (CCR) Anchor Standards—"broad standards" which complement the grade-specific CCSS (p. 10)—and the strategic processing actions Fountas and Pinnell outline in their seminal work, *Comprehending and Fluency: Thinking, Talking, and Writing About Reading, K–8* (2006).

CCR	Thinking Within the Text
Key Ideas and Details	Read closely to determine what the text says explicitly and make logical inferences from it; cite specific textual evidence when writing or speaking to support conclusions drawn from the text.
	Determine central ideas or themes of a text and analyze their development; summarize key supporting details and ideas.
	Analyze how and why individuals, events, and ideas develop and take place over the course of a text.
	Thinking Beyond the Text
Integration of Knowledge and Ideas	Integrate and evaluate content presented in diverse media and formats, including the validity of the reasoning as well as the relevance and sufficiency of the evidence.
	Delineate and evaluate the argument and specific claims in a text, including the validity of the reasoning as well as the relevance and sufficiency of the evidence.
	Analyze how two or more texts address similar themes or topics in order to build knowledge or to compare the approaches the authors take.
	Thinking About the Text
Craft and Structure	Interpret words and phrases as they are used in a text, including determining technical, connotative, and figurative meanings, and analyze how specific word choices shape meaning or tone.
	Analyze the structure of texts, including how specific sentences, paragraphs, and portions of the text, such as a section, chapter, scene, or stanza, relate to each other and the whole.
	Assess how point of view or purpose shapes the content and style of a text.

THE IMPORTANCE OF READING A
VARIETY OF TEXTS AND GENRES

Creating motivated readers is a challenge for any teacher faced with a class that varies widely in backgrounds, interests, and abilities. For students to become active readers, they must be exposed to a number and variety of texts and genres that are interesting and engaging, informative, accessible, representative of our diverse world, and include content appropriate for each student's age and gender. By selecting and introducing a variety of texts and genres over a period of time and demonstrating the many ways one can experience texts, you can help your students build a flexible reading process that will make any text accessible.

How do texts vary?

When students are exposed to a variety of good-quality texts within many genres, they can compare and connect texts across genres and become familiar with text characteristics. However, variety is more than an assortment of books of different genres. It includes format, special types of text across genres, different media, and a wide range of content and diversity.

Why is format important?

The sizes, shapes, designs, layouts, illustrations, binding, and placement and styles of print constitute some of the different formats in which text is presented. The types of formats students are most likely to encounter include fiction and nonfiction picture books, leveled readers, short stories, chapter books, series books, poems, short stories, short informational texts, magazines targeted to young readers, graphic novels, and comic books. Having available texts in different formats will increase opportunities for all students to find something they want to read. By experiencing texts in a wide range of formats, students also develop the ability to process different kinds of language and visual information.

How do genres vary?

Genre means types of text that are basically prose or poetry. Poetry comes in many forms, including traditional songs and rhymes, free verse, chants, and haiku. Prose can be divided into fiction and nonfiction, which is further divided into many types of text. Fiction can include realistic fiction, historical fiction, fantasy, science fiction, and traditional literature such as fables, folktales, and myths. Nonfiction includes biography, autobiography, memoirs, and informational, narrative, expository, and persuasive texts.

Why is genre important?

Different genres make different demands on readers. Students who are exposed to a wide variety of genres develop analytical-thinking skills and become more flexible in processing text. As their knowledge of genre grows, readers learn what to expect when they begin to read a text and can adjust their reading strategies accordingly. Even more important, they learn how to think within, beyond, and about their reading.

Through prose, students learn how language can be used to explain, describe, persuade, and elaborate. They become a part of the wider world, past and present, in nonfiction and enter imaginary worlds in fiction. They also discover how to think critically about what they read.

Why is diversity important?

Students also should be exposed to texts in both leveled books and books available for independent reading that reflect different cultures, languages, races, geographic regions, religions, and traditions. Through fiction and nonfiction texts that reflect our world, students will identify with characters in books and will learn about diversity, also learning to value it. In addition, they will discover viewpoints and perspectives that are different from their own.

How do different types of media help readers?

Providing variety in types of text is important in stretching students' thinking, but doing so also requires accessibility. Reading aloud varied texts gives all students quick and easy access to a wider range of genres and text levels they might not be ready to read independently. This same access can be provided with CDs and DVD movies based on books or stories. By making texts accessible to all students, you will have a basis for discussion that can involve the whole class.

Creating a Collection

When creating a classroom collection of books that will develop strong readers and writers and demand growth, remember to look for:

- **high-quality texts**
- **a variety of genres in fiction, nonfiction, and poetry**
- **favorite authors and illustrators**
- **enough copies for students' needs and your curriculum**
- **variety to interest students, both male and female**
- **variety in a range of reading levels**

Why Are Text Types Important?

As the old adage goes, "Variety is the spice of life." One decade inside the 21st century, however, access to a wide variety of genres, such as informational text, historical fiction, fables, folktales, adventure stories, and mysteries, and text types, such as picture books, chapter books, plays, and graphic novels, not only spice up our students' reading, but also provide a full and essential menu of the kind of challenging texts our students must learn to process and understand if they are to thrive in our complex world with its staggering array of textual offerings. Indeed, as classics scholar Jay David Bolter explains in his book *Writing Space (1993)*, literacy has always meant the capacity to use a society's most powerful tools to create and receive meaning. And today, those tools are electronic and multimodal in order to access text that, increasingly, is hypertexted. This means that within the context of one text, our students are following links and processing not only multiple texts, but also multiple genres in varied formats. Clearly, the wide reading of multiple text types and formats that guided reading promotes is invaluable.

The National Assessment of Educational Progress (NAEP) recognizes this reality and in 2009 developed matrixes for literary text that students need to know in the 21st century. While NAEP targets older students, Grades 4, 8, and 12, Irene Fountas and Gay Su Pinnell ask, "Why wait?" Even very young children are engaging with multiple forms of text every day as they figure out how to download a favorite video game, dip into the Sunday comics, or read email from a new pen pal in Ghana, and each textual encounter represents a unique reading challenge right from the very beginning of their reading careers. Children need to engage with many text types so they can learn each one's distinct language, content, and organizational patterns and structures. Through such engagement, students learn that different types of texts have different characteristics that require them to meet different challenges as readers. As Fountas and Pinnell note, *textual variety* leads to *flexible processing* (2006).

Guided Reading: Text Types provides not only the genres that correspond to the NAEP Literary Matrixes, but also the forms, or text types, including the following:

Picture Books	Series Books	Short Stories	Free Verse
Chapter Books	Graphic Novels	Plays	Novels

The Common Core State Standards and Text Types

While the CCSS expressly do not present a particular reading list, they do call for wide reading of varied text types that grow in complexity as children progress up the grade levels, a foundational principle of guided reading. The criteria the Standards outline for text selection reflect those used to create the *Scholastic Guided Reading Program.*

• **Complexity:** teachers typically match readers and texts in light of particular academic tasks; therefore, texts must be of sufficient complexity at each grade level based on both quantitative and qualitative measures.

• **Quality:** the Standards call for "classic or historically significant texts as well as contemporary works of comparable literary merit, cultural significance, and rich content" across genres.

• **Breadth:** the Standards require as broad a range of sufficiently complex, high-quality texts as possible and consider such factors as initial publication date, authorship, and subject matter, variables that also influenced the selection of text types.

In sum, in effective reading instruction, text types count. Our developing readers must encounter "a wide range of text structures," and teachers must be "explicit in the purposes for, and uses of, texts" (Kucer, 2008, Hoffman, et al., 2000).

GENRE/TEXT TYPE
DESCRIPTIONS AND KEY FEATURES

The *Scholastic Guided Reading Program* provides a wide variety of fiction and nonfiction genres and text types.

FICTION

Realistic Fiction

Realistic fiction tells a story that could possibly happen to real people. The characters appear to have problems and goals that real people have, and attempt to solve these problems or reach goals with plausible actions. Readers often experience realistic fiction as truthful and can identify with and see themselves in the characters.

Key Features

- believable characters with human problems and desires
- setting that reflects real places and time
- character-driven events
- reasonable outcomes that reflect real life
- humor may be an element

Mystery

A mystery is a special type of fiction that centers on a problem that needs to be solved. The problem can be missing or stolen objects, puzzles, criminals to be identified and caught, and strange behavior that needs to be explained. Suspense and sometimes danger and fear play an important part in the action.

Key Features

- characters involved in solving a problem such as a puzzle or crime
- setting may be mysterious or ordinary
- plot carries the story as characters follow clues to solve the mystery
- mood is suspenseful
- familiar forms are detective stories, strange adventures, and tales of espionage and crime.

Historical Fiction

Realistic fiction that takes place in the past is considered historical fiction. The story combines imagination and fact with characters as part of a fictional plot placed in a real historical setting. The setting is often integral to the plot as it affects how characters live and act as well as the events they are a part of.

Key Features

- believable characters
- setting that reflects a historical time and place
- details of how people live and work fit the time and place
- real historical people may appear as characters although what they do and say may be fictional unless historically documented

| **Fantasy** | Fantasy includes stories that are not possible in real life. Characters or settings may be imaginary, or the events and characters' actions or abilities are not realistic. Once readers willingly accept the fantasy, the characters may be plausible with realistic problems, and the outcome may be reasonable. |

Key Features

- characters may be imaginary, have magical abilities, and/or include personified animals
- settings may be imaginary and change as characters travel through time or move into alternate worlds
- plot may involve a conflict between good and evil

Science Fiction

Science fiction is a type of fantasy that tells about events that have not happened yet or that could not happen in real life as it is known today. The imaginary elements are technology-driven instead of magical. The science established in a science fiction story may not be explained, but it must remain consistent to be believable.

Key Features

- stories may take place in outer space, on other worlds, or in alternate dimensions
- science and technology are used to create a world or characters that are not possible in present real life
- the setting is usually important to the story as it affects characters and their actions

Traditional Literature

Traditional literature encompasses stories that have been passed down orally through many generations. Different versions of the same tale often appear in many cultures. Readers expect recurring themes and structures, such as three wishes, journeys or quests, tricksters, or heroes who are often young.

Key Features

- **Folktale:** an often humorous story that comes from a particular culture and is told orally until it is eventually recorded; includes stock characters that fill one function, simple conflicts and goals, fast action, repetitive events often in threes, and a definitive outcome
- **Fable:** a brief story, usually with animal characters, that teaches a moral or a lesson that is stated clearly at the end of the story
- **Fairy Tale:** a short story with magical characters and events; characters are usually all good or all bad; repetition in characters and actions; often begins with "once upon a time" and ends with "and they lived happily ever after"; has a more elaborate structure than a folktale

Adventure	An adventure tells a story that involves characters in exciting, and often risky, situations. Characters may accomplish heroic feats.
Key Features	• setting may be real or imaginary • plot may involve danger • stories may take place in other times and places

NONFICTION

Informational Text	Informational text provides factual information. Content may be scientific or social, exploring the natural and physical world or people and places in the past or present. Informational text can be presented in a variety of formats including reference books, books on specific subjects or processes, magazines, CDs, or filmed documentaries.
Key Features	• provides information on a whole class of things, places, or people • describes and explains • compares and contrasts • includes technical vocabulary • often includes headings and subheadings to divide text • presents information through graphics such as photographs, charts, diagrams, and maps as well as text • includes labels and captions • includes a table of contents and an index • may include a bibliography
Biography/Autobiography	A biography or an autobiography is about a single historical or current person. It may cover the person's whole life or a significant period. An autobiography is written by the person who is the subject of the story. An autobiography may take the form of a memoir in which the person relates his or her experiences during a meaningful time. A biography is written by an author about a person who is the subject of the book.
Key Features	• covers one person's life or a significant period of that person's life • usually written about an important person • may include photographs and illustrations • may include a table of contents, an index, and/or a bibliography

TEXT TYPES

Picture Book	A picture book has illustrations that help tell the story or photos to convey information.
Key Features	• pictures show characters, setting, and plot in fictional text • photographs and graphics help provide content in informational text
Play	A play is a story that is intended to be performed. Plays are character-driven, as they are told through what the characters say and do.
Key Features	• written in dialogue form with character names identifying the speaker • includes character actions and expressions briefly indicated, usually parenthetically • may include one or more acts with a clearly identified setting • usually includes in the beginning a list of characters and their characteristics such as name, age, and identity or profession
Chapter Book/Novel	A chapter book is a work of fiction that contains all story elements, including characters, setting, plot, and theme. A novel is a longer work. Because of its longer length, a novel can more fully develop characters over time and place. The length of a novel requires readers to develop reading stamina and the ability to follow plots and characters over an extended period of time and several reading sessions.
Key Features	• story is usually divided into chapters • may include several major and minor characters that are fully developed • may include story background in the beginning or as the story unfolds • may include several subplots • plot may include many events as action rises and falls • may include a resolution and events after the climax or turning point
Graphic Novel	Graphic novels are similar to comic books, but they tell a more complete story with a beginning, middle, and end. A graphic novel often resembles a novel in length and narrative. The term *graphic* refers to the pictorial nature of the novel.
Key Features	• story told through pictures • dialogue included in speech balloons • narrative may be within story frames or at the top of a page • characters developed through dialogue and illustration
Short Stories	A short story is a short work of fiction that includes the story elements of characters, setting, plot, and theme.
Key Features	• usually is a part of a collection • may be any fictional genre

INCLUDING **NONFICTION AND INFORMATIONAL TEXT** IN PRIMARY CLASSROOMS

adapted from *Reading & Writing Informational Text in the Primary Grades*
(Duke and Bennett-Armistead, 2003)

Guided Reading: Text Types includes a variety of nonfiction and informational texts as part of its genre array. Often the terms "informational text" and "nonfiction" are used interchangeably, but they are not the same. Informational text is a type of nonfiction—a very important type. Nonfiction includes any text that is factual. (Or, by some definitions, any type of literature that is factual, which would exclude text such as menus and street signs.) Informational text differs from other types of nonfiction in that its primary purpose is to convey information about the natural or social world, and typically includes particular linguistic features such as headings and technical vocabulary.

It is important to note that within informational text, there are several different types of text that might be considered informational text genres or subgenres including:

- **reference books such as encyclopedias, field guides, and so on**
- **"all about" books, on topics such as spiders or dinosaurs**
- **process-informational books including books about how an animal develops from conception to adulthood or about how some substance is created or transformed**
- **magazines, newspapers, posters, pamphlets, websites, CD-ROMs, and so on**

Why focus on informational and nonfiction texts in primary classrooms? There are a number of arguments for doing so. Some of these arguments have a more solid research base than others, and some may be more compelling than others. But the research available to this point is clear. Students need to encounter more informational text because:

Informational Text Is Key to Success in Later Schooling

We have all heard that from around fourth grade on, "reading to learn" is a major focus in school (Chall, 1983). Students encounter more textbooks and other forms of informational text as they move through the grades. The tests they take contain increasingly more difficult informational texts. If teachers include more informational text in early schooling, they put students in a better position to handle the reading and writing demands of their later schooling.

Informational Text Is Ubiquitous in Society

Several studies have looked at the kinds of things people write *outside* of school—what students and adults read and write in their workplaces, homes, and communities. Again and again these studies have shown that adults read a great deal of nonfiction, including informational text (e.g., Venezky, 1982; Smith, 2000). This is not likely to change and, in fact, in our increasingly information-based economy, it may only increase. According to one study (Kamil & Lane, 1998), 96 percent of the text on the World Wide Web is expository.

Informational Text Is Preferred Reading Material for Many Students

When researchers investigate the kinds of texts students like to read, they've found that different students have different reading preferences. Some students seem to prefer informational text, some seem to prefer narrative text, and many don't seem to have preferences for any particular genre. For those students who prefer informational text—students that Ron Jobe and Mary Dayton-Sakari (2002) call "Info-Kids"—including more informational text in classrooms may improve attitudes toward reading and even serve as a catalyst for overall literacy development (Caswell & Duke, 1998).

Informational Text Builds Knowledge of the Natural and Social Worlds

By definition, informational text conveys information about the natural and social worlds (Duke, 2000). Reading and listening to informational text therefore can develop students' knowledge of that world (e.g., Anderson & Guthrie, 1999; Duke & Kays, 1998). This in turn can promote students' comprehension of subsequent texts they read (e.g., Wilson & Anderson, 1986), because it can build background knowledge.

Young Children Can Handle Informational Text

The research is clear. Young children *can* interact successfully with informational text. (See Dreher, 2000; Duke, 2003; and Duke, Bennett-Armistead, & Roberts, 2002, 2003, for reviews of research on this point.) Studies show that Kindergartners can develop knowledge of information-book language and content from information-book read alouds and shared readings. Primary-grade students can comprehend informational text that they read themselves. Research also indicates that young children can write informational text. So you needn't worry that informational text is inherently "over the heads" of your students, and you should be able to respond with confidence to colleagues who have doubts.

THINKING WITHIN, BEYOND, AND ABOUT THE TEXT

Adapted from *Teaching for Comprehending and Fluency: Thinking, Talking, and Writing About Reading, K-8* (Irene C. Fountas and Gay Su Pinnell, 2006)

When proficient readers process a text, they simultaneously draw on a wide range of strategic actions that are physical, emotional, cognitive, and linguistic. As students learn the skills and strategies they need to make sense of a text, this process becomes more effective and automatic. Eventually, the reading process becomes unconscious. In order to reach this point, students need to learn how proficient readers think about reading. Teachers may often interpret this as making sure students comprehend what they are reading. However, checking for comprehension by asking endless questions during reading can turn into an interrogation that interferes with the reading process. Having students learn and focus on one reading strategy at a time also can make the reading process less effective. Instead, students need guidance in how to integrate strategic actions and use them effectively with many kinds of texts. For the teacher, this means knowing what readers must be able to do and the information they need to access to process a text.

Readers access a wide range of information that is both visible and invisible. Visible information is what students see as words and art in the text. As they read, readers recognize letters, words, punctuation, format, and text structures, and they attach meaning to what they see. Proficient readers are barely aware of this processing of visual information as they focus on meaning. Invisible information—including the knowledge and experience of language, facts, and the world both past and present—is what readers know and think about as they respond to visual information. Such personal knowledge is different for each student and is shaped by family, culture, and community. As students learn about different cultures and communities, they expand their perspectives and make new connections. Many of the texts they encounter can become the basis for this expansion.

Another form of invisible information is readers' experiences with many kinds of text, including knowledge of genres, text structures, and formats. This knowledge helps readers form expectations and predictions about a new text, access meaning as they read, and respond to the text after reading.

Different kinds of texts make different demands on readers. Texts that students can read independently help them build their knowledge. Texts that students can read with teacher support challenge them to develop new strategic actions for reading. You can help students meet these demands by giving them opportunities to think about their reading within, beyond, and about text.

Thinking Within the Text

When readers think within the text, they gather basic information from the text and determine its basic meaning. To do so, readers must process the text by:

- **decoding words and using word meaning and what they know about language**
- **searching for information, and noting and sorting important details**
- **determining how the text is organized**
- **monitoring themselves for accuracy and understanding**
- **adjusting reading speed and technique according to the type of text**
- **sustaining fluency**

Understanding the basic meaning of a text forms the foundation for higher thinking skills. By thinking within the text, readers can gather important information and summarize what they have read.

Thinking Beyond the Text

When readers think beyond the text, they go more deeply into its meaning beyond their literal understanding of it. They are able to:

- **make predictions**
- **connect their reading to their own experiences**
- **relate the text to similar texts**
- **integrate what they know with new information**
- **infer ideas that are not directly stated**
- **think about the greater meaning of the text**

Thinking beyond the text allows readers to understand character motivations, explore how setting influences the story, and follow more complex plots. They also identify and learn new information that they can incorporate into what they already know and understand.

Thinking About the Text

To think about the text, readers analyze and critique what they read. They examine a text to:

- **note how it is constructed**
- **note how the writer uses language**
- **identify literary devices**
- **determine how the writer has provided information, such as using compare and contrast, description, or cause and effect**
- **identify characteristics of the genre**
- **use their own knowledge to think critically about ideas**
- **evaluate quality and authenticity**

Thinking about the text helps readers move beyond identifying likes and dislikes and helps them learn more about how texts work. It also helps them better appreciate different genres, good-quality writing, and their own writing.

Guiding Students to Think Within, Beyond, and About the Text

Thinking about the text is a complex process that is difficult to teach or demonstrate. Although there is value in directing readers to important aspects of the text, effective reading strategies should be shown as working together in an integrated process. You can talk about the text before reading, at certain points during reading, and after reading to motivate questions and ideas. You can share your own ideas and demonstrate the different kinds of thinking readers do. However, instruction must still allow readers to respond to the text in a way that expands and expresses their own thinking.

In your guided reading groups, you can help your students learn how to think within, beyond, and about the text by being mindful of:

- **the important aspects of processing related to reading the texts you have selected**
- **what you want your students to do**
- **the learning opportunities presented by a particular text**
- **how students might respond to text features that could open opportunities for teaching**

What follows are some tips about how to help students think within, beyond, and about fiction and nonfiction texts.

Fiction

To think within the text, help students to:

- **follow the events of the plot; show how to think about what happens first, then next**
- **gather information about characters and setting by giving examples of what to look for**
- **learn about the characters by noting how they are described, what they say or think, what others say about them, and how they change over the course of the story**
- **identify the conflict or problem, and the solution**
- **solve words by thinking about their meaning in context**

To think beyond the text, help students to:

- **infer character motivations and feelings by looking for evidence in the text and by making connections between themselves and the characters**
- **infer why characters change over time by looking for evidence in the story**
- **connect the text to background knowledge, personal experiences, and other texts by thinking about other stories the text reminds them of, what they already know about the topic, place, or time, and how the plot or characters are similar to another text**
- **predict how the problem is solved by thinking about what has happened, what will happen next, and what is known about the characters**
- **understand the theme or message by thinking about what the writer is trying to say**
- **relate the theme, plot, or characters to their own lives**
- **infer how events are significant**
- **note new ideas, identify how their thinking has changed and what they have learned**

To think about the text, help students to:

- evaluate the importance of the setting by thinking how the text would be different if set in another time or place, or how the story changed when the setting changed
- notice how the writer made the characters realistic
- pay attention to the plot structure by thinking about how the story is organized, how the writer shows the passing of time, and identifying any flashbacks
- note aspects of the writer's craft by looking for language that helped them clarify something
- evaluate the quality or authenticity of the text

Nonfiction

To think within the text, help students to:

- gather and remember important information by deciding what they will learn from the text and what they think is important
- gather and remember information from the illustrations and graphics
- use different tools, such as a table of contents, headings, captions, index, and glossary, to locate and use information

To think beyond the text, help students to:

- identify new information and add it to their existing knowledge by thinking how their ideas might have changed after reading the text
- make connections between the text and background knowledge, personal experience, and other texts by thinking what the text reminds them of and what they already knew about the topic
- infer cause and effect by thinking about what happened and why
- identify the problem and the solution posed by the writer
- notice and understand the sequence of events
- analyze description by examining details and looking for examples in the text

To think about the text, help students to:

- recognize if and how the writer uses cause and effect, problem and solution, description, sequence, and compare and contrast by noticing how the writer constructed the story
- evaluate the authenticity and accuracy of the text by thinking about why the text seems accurate and how facts could be checked
- decide how the writer made the topic interesting by looking for specific examples
- analyze why the writer chose particular information to include in graphics

THE IMPORTANCE OF TALKING ABOUT BOOKS

Discussing books should be a rich part of every student's reading life. When students are encouraged and given opportunities to talk about books with peers and their teachers, they become motivated to share what they liked best about a text—and what they found interesting or surprising. They learn how to ask questions to find out what other students thought about a text and how to recommend a favorite book. They experience having their opinions valued rather than evaluated. They also discover that talking about books is fun.

Getting students to talk about books beyond the usual "I liked it" or "I didn't like it" or short answers to questions about specific texts is often difficult. However, there are a variety of ways you can spark discussion about books in your classroom including book clubs, literature circles, and topic discussions.

Interactive Read-Aloud

Before students can effectively discuss books with others, they need to learn how to talk about books. You can help them learn by conducting interactive read-alouds in which you demonstrate how to talk about books. Begin by selecting a text you know your students will enjoy, or invite them to select a text from several you offer. After you introduce the text, read it aloud and pause occasionally to demonstrate how to talk about the book. Then invite students to join in. Students can share comments or questions or respond to a discussion prompt with the whole group, another student, or a small group. After reading, you can invite students to comment on what the text means, link it to other books, reflect on the writer's craft, and evaluate text quality.

During an interactive read-aloud, students learn how to:

- **focus on the text**
- **use suitable words when talking about a text**
- **listen actively and respect others' ideas**
- **build on others' comments**
- **back up their opinions with evidence from the text**

Through active participation, students learn that they are expected to respond to one another's comments and that everyone should participate.

Literature Discussion Groups

Once students have learned how to talk about books, they can try out their skills in literature discussion groups. These small groups, each consisting of four to six students, operate under many different names including book clubs, literature circles, and topic discussions. They all are organized around students sharing their thinking about texts.

In literature discussion groups, students are in charge of their own thinking, talking, and writing. They have a chance to share what they think within, beyond, and about a text. As a result, interest in their own learning grows.

At first, you will need to be closely involved with book clubs and literature circles to set routines and select books. Choose books that are developmentally appropriate as well as interesting. Have a copy for each student in a group. Be sure that everyone in the class is a part of a discussion group. A group can consist of students who are interested in a particular author, topic, or genre. Some groups might be all girls or all boys.

Designate where and when book clubs will meet. Encourage members to come prepared by having read the selected book and spending some time thinking about it, deciding on information and ideas to share. Have students sit in a circle at a table or on the floor so they can see one another. You may want to post a list of text elements for fiction and nonfiction for the group to refer to as they discuss the book. Book club meetings will normally last about fifteen minutes for younger students and up to thirty minutes for older, more experienced students.

You can participate by helping groups get their discussions started, move beyond a sticking point, or continue when they think they have run out of things to say. Note how group members work with each other, and be sure they give evidence for their opinions from the text or personal experience. Encourage them to ask questions, especially when they don't understand something. As students become more experienced in discussing books, you can move gradually into the role of observer, interacting with groups only as needed.

As you observe book discussions, pay attention to both process and content. Some groups may be proficient at the process of talking about a book but not about the content, so they end up saying little about the deeper meaning of a book. The purpose of a book club is for students to learn how to explore the meaning of a text and express their thinking about that text. Other groups may have many ideas to share, but they don't know how to organize their meeting. You may need to spend some time with these groups to remind them how to lead a discussion, let everyone have a turn, listen when others are speaking, and participate in the discussion.

CONNECTING TO
EVERYDAY LITERACY

Consider the way in which you relish a 400-page beach book, or confront the programming instructions for your new smart phone, or peruse the cable menu for your favorite nighttime show. While you may be using the same basic cognitive strategies to process the text, you make numerous unconscious adjustments based on what you are reading and for what purpose. Research on the nature of text and on reading processes explains why these adjustments are needed: "the characteristics of literary and informational text differ dramatically" (NAEP 2009 Reading Framework, p. 7). In other words, it is no longer enough to simply focus on our reading instruction; we need to pay careful attention to the nature of the text we are asking our students to read, understanding that they must adjust their reading processes to accommodate the differences among the texts they encounter in our classrooms and in the world beyond. Fountas and Pinnell (2008) explain:

> At all levels, readers may slow down to problem solve words or complex language and resume a normal pace, although at higher levels this process is mostly unobservable. Readers make adjustments as they search for information; they may reread, search graphics or illustrations, go back to specific references in the text, or use specific readers' tools. At all levels, readers also adjust expectations and ways of reading according to purpose, genre, and previous reading experiences. At early levels, readers have only beginning experiences to draw on, but at more advanced levels, they have rich resources in terms of the knowledge of genre (p. 225).

Why Everyday Print Belongs on Your Guided Reading Table

We have long known that children as young as three years of age (and younger) are noticing the print and print graphics in our environment and interacting with it. Increasingly, our lives are governed by maps, menus, memos, and mail, both so-called snail and digital. This just represents a fraction of our daily print and electronic bombardment. Given the ubiquitous nature of everyday print, and the fact it carries its own strategic processing actions, as well as the rise of time spent on the computer, the occasion is long overdue to bring everyday print to classrooms and to guided reading tables and help our students appreciate and process it as its own unique genre and text type.

Alignment With the NAEP

For nearly four decades, the National Assessment of Education Progress (NAEP) has been measuring the academic achievement of U.S. elementary and secondary students—helping to define and evaluate their condition and progress. It is not surprising, then, that the NAEP also offers guidance on the sorts of text our students should read as we move into the new world of the 21st century. The NAEP literary matrices target Grades 4, 8, and 12. *Guided Reading: Text Types* focuses on younger children, Grades K–6, to prepare them for reading literature to build the literacy and comprehension skills they will need throughout their schooling careers and beyond. All of the genres and text types in *Guided Reading: Text Types* align with NAEP's Literary Text matrices. But you will find another major bonus as well. Some of the writing activities and *Connecting to Everyday Literacy* features on the back of every teaching card connect students to real-world text that aligns to NAEP's Informational Text matrices for the following:

1. **Exposition**—presenting information, providing explanations and definitions, and comparing and contrasting

2. **Procedural Texts and Documents**—conveying information in the form of directions for accomplishing a task. Composed of discrete steps to be performed in a sequence. How-to graphical representations: tables, application forms, lists, pie graphs, maps, etc.

3. **Argumentation and Persuasive**—seeking to influence through appeals that direct readers to specific goals or try to win them to specific beliefs; editorials, advertisements, brochures, etc.

The feature *Connecting to Everyday Literacy*, which you will find on the back of every teaching card, links the content of a trade book or an element of a trade book to a kind of real-world text. For example, if your students are reading historical fiction and they come across a reference to a map in the book, *Connecting to Everyday Literacy* may link them to maps. You can see the advantages: within the meaningful context of an engaging story or informational text, your students have the opportunity to explore and exercise their cognitive processing strategies across such practical, real-world texts as bus schedules, recipes, and instruction manuals. Plus, there is a website link that you can share with your students that shows more real-world procedural, persuasive, or expository text.

In addition, Fountas and Pinnell have developed a separate program called *Everyday Literacy* that provides students and teachers with a variety of everyday texts to engage with and explore—both in print and on CD ROM. Grade-level, thematically linked sets provide whole-class instruction suitable for any guided reading classroom.

EXPOSITION, PERSUASION, AND PROCEDURAL TEXT

The pen is mightier than the sword and, indeed, our nation was founded on, and saved again and again, sometimes on little more than the sheer power of exposition, persuasion, and procedural texts. These are text types our students must learn to control as they make up the bulk of what we read outside of school and, increasingly, inside school as well. The *Guided Reading Program* showcases and links students in Grades K–6 to exposition, persuasion, and procedural text—giving them a jump start on developing the high-powered cognitive strategies students need to process and control these texts effectively.

Research suggests that students typically do not learn the comprehension strategies needed to fully process informational texts without the support of explicit teaching (Dymock, 2005). This may account for the struggles some students experience as they attempt to understand textbooks filled with content-specific vocabulary, textual features, and procedural displays. Without specific how-to-read-a-textbook instruction, some students may become lost and give up. While most students are comfortable with the familiar structure of literary texts and their elements of theme, plot, conflict and resolution, characters and setting, informational texts offer a whole new set of elements and patterns.

Exposition

Exposition presents information, provides explanations and definitions, and comes in a variety of patterns, such as description, sequence, compare-contrast, cause-effect, and problem-solution. Since expository text conveys factual information, students may struggle with unfamiliar vocabulary and concepts, and encounter ideas that have little to do with their own personal experiences. Jim Burke (2002) outlines our teaching task:

> Students need to know how expository texts work, how they should prepare to read them, and what to do once they begin reading such texts. Expository texts include essays, speeches, journals, government documents, newspaper and magazine articles. While each type of text shares certain characteristics with the others, they each make their own demands on the reader through the unique use of structure, devices, features, and conventions. We need to teach students how to read each type as they encounter it if they are to read them successfully (p. x, 2004).

Expository text is defined, in part, by its textual structure—the ways in which ideas are interrelated so as to convey meaning to readers. Identifying these unique structures may be the first step to comprehending and controlling expository text. During guided reading, teachers can introduce the structures that help define expository text:

Problem-Solution—the text presents a problem, offers solutions, and leads the reader to the most viable one.

Description—the text provides specific details about a topic, person, event, or idea.

Cause-and-Effect—the text links events or effects with their causes. Watch for the *causal indicators* that signal a cause-and-effect relationship such as *because, for,* and *since.*

Enumeration or Categorizing—as the name suggests, the text is organized by means of lists or by collecting together like items.

Sequencing—the text is organized in terms of time or an ordered progression, i.e., the actions that led to an historical event or the steps in a scientific process. Watch for signal words such as *first, second, last, earlier, later, now, then, next, after, during,* and *finally.*

Compare and Contrast—the text showcases differences and similarities between two or more topics, which may include ideas, people, locations, and events. Watch for signal words, such as *like, as, still, although, yet, but, however,* and *on the other hand.*

Persuasion

Our goal as teachers is to help our students understand persuasion from the inside out so they can control its influence on themselves and use it effectively to frame and promote their own ideas. It doesn't take much to engage children in big ideas and get them reading, writing, thinking, and debating passionately and persuasively—and using the needed strategic processing actions best acquired through guided reading. Imagine the persuasive text and talk that might erupt as children consider all aspects of a text.

While expository text seeks to inform and educate, persuasive text angles to persuade and influence. Again, students will encounter language, ideas, content, and structures that may not be familiar to them unless they are introduced to these texts at the guided reading table. Here's an opportunity to consider the author's voice: does it help or hinder? Stylistic features: appeal or repel? Language: soar and hook, or flop and bore? In other words, in the hands of a master writer, even a dull topic like what kind of insect repellent is the best to buy can buzz. A persuasive passage offers opportunities to crack open text and study what makes it work: vital, absorbing prose, personality and pizzazz, vivid examples, humor, irony, surprise—all can work together to create a persuasive text that delights. In the process of deconstructing such text in order to analyze and appreciate its virtues, students learn about how to construct their own. As students will come to understand, there's a reason it's called the *art* of persuasion.

Procedural Text

It has become a matter of survival—nearly every household has a designated reader who gamely tackles the manuals that accompany every gadget in the home. Someone has to read the manual so you can program your microwave oven, set your porch lights to go on at nightfall, or upgrade your photo sharing software. These manuals are the procedural texts that enable us to function in our tech-charged world, and they now seem to permeate our every waking moment. Consider a morning newspaper: if read online, a reader is no longer simply reading journalistic prose; he or she hops from link to link that may include pie charts, graphs, maps, and statistical charts. By some estimates, we may spend more time reading documents and information in matrix form than we do reading extended prose. Try getting through the day without reading some sort of procedural text—schedules, catalogs, directions. Chances are you won't succeed. And even though much of this material is extra textual elements tucked inside another text that serve to guide the reader through the original text—titles, labels, headings, subheadings, sidebars, charts, graphs, legends, and the like—it's essential text, more than deserving of instructional time at guided reading tables.

USING THE TEACHING CARDS

Each card provides teachers with a quick and essential analysis of the book students will read.

The Good Dog

Summary & Standard

McKinley is the top dog in town, but his authority is challenged when a dog is abused by its owner and a wolf arrives to recruit dogs back to the wild. Students will distinguish fantasy from reality.

Author: Avi
Genre: Fantasy
Text Type: Chapter Book

Word Count: 250+
Theme/Idea: overcoming obstacles; standing up for what you believe in

Meets standards and makes real-world connections.

Making Connections: Text to World

A dog is the narrator in the story, but the setting and situations are realistic. Ask students who have dogs to explain how their pets communicate with them and how the dogs are trained to behave in certain ways.

Extend the connection by pointing out that dogs and wolves are related and share many behaviors. However, wolves are wild animals and are endangered. This is often due to conflicts between humans and wolves. Point out that it is important to understand the behavior of wolves in order to protect them.

For more information about wolves, see http://nationalzoo.si.edu/Animals/NorthAmerica/Facts/fact-graywolf.cfm.

Builds rich oral and written vocabulary.

Vocabulary

Essential Words: appreciation, bounding, frustration, reverberated, submission, tentative

Related Words for Discussion: endangered, responsibility, survival

Genre/Text Type

Fantasy/Chapter Book Remind students that a fantasy is a story that could not happen in the real world. The story unfolds with each new chapter.

Supportive Book Features

Text The book has large type, widely spaced lines, and short chapters that make the text easy to read. The author describes certain dog behaviors and explains what each means. Questions at the end of the book will spark further discussion.

Vocabulary Students will find the book's vocabulary easy to comprehend. The more difficult words that the author does not define within the text can be decoded easily using context clues.

Praise students for specific use of "Behaviors to Notice and Support" on page 114 of the *Guided Reading Teacher's Guide*.

Challenging Book Features

Text Make sure students realize that the human characters cannot understand what the dogs are saying even though the dogs' thoughts are shown as dialogue for the reader.

Content Students will need to pay attention to clues in the story to help them understand the action and the characters' feelings. Because the dogs have human names and dialogue, it is often hard to distinguish between the humans and dogs. Have students keep a list of characters as they encounter them in the story.

LEVEL S

ELL Bridge

Explain to students that McKinley lacks the vocabulary for certain objects and places. He uses descriptive phrases instead. Point out phrases McKinley uses in place of certain words, such as *tall bowls* (drinking glasses), *eating sticks* (silverware), and *glow box* (TV). Help students record in a three-column chart each term in "dog language," in English, and in their home language.

Easily adapts lessons to meet the needs of English language learners.

SCHOLASTIC

Helps students think within, beyond, and about each text to enhance comprehension.

Builds the reading skills identified by the **National Reading Panel** and reading experts.

Teaching Options

Developing Comprehension

Thinking Within the Text
Have students identify the problems that McKinley feels are his duty to solve. (the abuse faced by Duchess, the wolf's presence, Redburn's challenge to McKinley's leadership, and the pup's desire to run away with the wolf) Discuss how these problems are connected and how the solution to one problem also solves another problem.

Thinking Beyond the Text
Have students think about how the author includes a message about the treatment of dogs and wolves as part of the plot. Ask: *What do you learn about pet care after reading about Duchess's dilemma?* (Dogs need exercise, love, and proper care.) *How does Lupin's injury make the reader more aware of the dangers wolves face?* (People often hurt wolves out of fear.)

Thinking About the Text
Have students notice how the author builds suspense at the end of chapters. The author hints at something that may happen or sets up a situation that needs to be resolved. The effect is that readers want to keep reading. Reread pages 50–51 and discuss what happens to make readers want to continue. (The wolf is on the trail coming straight toward them.)

Visualizing
Tell students that an author's choice of words helps readers visualize, or picture, what a scene looks like. Vivid words and descriptions help readers picture a scene in their minds.

- Have students reread page 77 and identify how the author describes McKinley's actions. Ask: *How do these actions show McKinley's intelligence?*

- Have students reread pages 95–96. Ask: *Why is this description more effective than merely saying that the wolf attacked the humans?*

For more prompts and ideas for teaching problem-solving strategies, see page 54 of the *Guided Reading Teacher's Guide.*

Developing Phonics and Word-Solving Strategies

Strong Verbs
Remind students that verbs tell what action occurs. Strong verbs help readers visualize the action by describing it more precisely.

- Read aloud page 112. Ask students to listen for verbs that describe how characters speak to each other. (barked, growled, whimpered) Discuss how each verb helps students more clearly picture each character's actions. Then have partners read page 121 and note strong verbs that help them picture the action of this scene.

Developing Fluency
Read aloud a page, modeling how fluent readers pay attention to punctuation and chunk phrases, and adjust their pace. Then have partners take turns reading aloud a page to each other.

Oral Language/Conversation
Talk About Endangered Animals Lead a discussion about how human contact with wild animals can often endanger the animals.

Extending Meaning Through Writing
- Have students write a small brochure that explains certain dog behaviors and what people should do in response. **(Expository)**

- Have students rewrite a scene from another character's point of view. **(Narrative)**

Extends meaning through writing and expanded reading lists.

Connecting to Everyday Literacy

In the story, Jack has read a lot about wolves and thinks he has spotted one. To link students to real-world expository text, share a feature article about wolves, preferably one that includes photographs or diagrams. Point out how this information might help students distinguish a wolf from a dog. For more expository text about wolves, go to http://www.pbs.org/wgbh/nova/wolves.

Connects the literature selection to expository, persuasive, or procedural text.

GRTTS05

PROMPTS TO SUPPORT
PROBLEM-SOLVING STRATEGIES

adapted from *Guided Reading: Good First Teaching for All Children* (Fountas and Pinnell, 1996)

Throughout a guided reading session, the teacher prompts, encourages and confirms students' attempts at problem solving. The teacher helps students apply the in-the-head strategies they already know to new text. The teacher also helps students use a variety of strategies as they read. The key is to prompt with just the right amount of support so that eventually, each student will take over the strategizing for herself.

Prompts to Support Early Readers
- Read it with your finger.
- Try _____. Would that make sense?/Would that sound right?
- Do you think it looks like _____?
- Can you find _____? (a known or new word)
- Did you have enough (or too many) words?
- Read that again and start the word.
- Did it match?
- Did you run out of words?

Prompts to Support a Reader's Self-Monitoring Strategies
- Were you right?
- Why did you stop?
- What letter would you expect to see at the beginning? At the end?
- Would _____ fit there?/make sense?
- Check it. Does it look and sound right to you?
- What did you notice? (after hesitation or stop)
- Could it be _____?
- It could be _____, but look at _____.
- You almost got that. See if you can find what is wrong.

Prompts to Support a Reader's Use of All Sources of Information

- Check the picture.
- Does that sound right?
- You said (_____). Does that make sense?
- What's wrong with this? (Repeat what the student said.)
- Try that again and think what would make sense.
- What could you try?
- What can you do to help yourself?
- Try that again and think what would sound right.
- Do you know a word like that?

Prompts to Support a Reader's Self-Correction

- Something wasn't quite right.
- I like the way you worked that out.
- You're nearly right. Try that again.

Prompts to Support Phrased, Fluent Reading

- Can you read this quickly?
- Put your words together so it sounds like talking.

ASSESSMENT
OBSERVATION

Overview

We define assessment as the collection of information about a student's learning, and evaluation as the judgment about the student's strengths and specific needs based on this information. Assessment should be continuous—based on observation and informal measures of reading performance. Evaluation should provide a guide for teaching decisions that will help the student's learning.

To assess and evaluate a student's literacy development, information needs to be collected to demonstrate the following:

- **how a student uses and responds to oral language in various settings.**
- **what a student knows about reading and writing.**
- **how a student uses reading and writing in various settings.**
- **how a student values reading and writing.**

The Guided Reading Program is structured to give information on different kinds of literacy skills for students with varied learning needs. The program supports literacy development in reading, writing, listening, and speaking. These literacy activities provide a wealth of assessment information.

Purposes of Assessment

As a student progresses from a beginning reader and writer to a fluent reader and writer, assessment may have several purposes:

- **to establish what a student initially knows about literacy.**
- **to identify a student's instructional reading level.**
- **to monitor a student's pattern of strengths.**
- **to establish a student's facility with informational text.**

Assessment needs to take place at the beginning of the school year to know what foundational skills students have and to identify potential skill needs. All school-age students know something about oral and written language and are ready to learn more. Some may have knowledge about environmental print but little experience with books or with writing. Others may be confident with books and with some writing.

Observation

One of the best ways to assess an individual student's learning is through observation. For a well-rounded view of the student, try to observe him or her throughout the day in a variety of settings, such as during small-group and whole-class instruction, during independent reading time, or in the classroom library. What exactly can you observe?

Some suggestions include:

- **oral language ability**
- **attitudes**
- **choices during "free time"**
- **specific behaviors related to print**
- **interests**
- **book-handling behaviors**
- **peer relationships**

Ask yourself questions such as the following when observing a student's behaviors related to print:

- **When the student reads or works with print, does he or she approach the task confidently?**
- **Does the student have a strategy for attempting unfamiliar words in reading and writing?**
- **Does the student read and write for different purposes?**
- **Can the student retell what he or she reads in a logical order?**
- **Does the student select reading materials suited to his or her personal interests?**
- **Does the student select reading materials suited to his or her level of reading development?**

Answers to these kinds of questions will help you make instructional decisions and set goals for an individual student, and will help the student progress in learning.

Make your observations systematic rather than random. Decide whom to focus on. Select one student or several at a time to closely watch. Keep a record for each student, noting what you see by recording it on self-adhesive stickies or peel-off labels that can be attached to the student's personal folder. Alternatively, keep a class list for easy referral.

When behaviors are observed, a check (✓) may be used. You may also wish to make a slash (/) the first time the behavior is observed and convert the slash to an X when you feel the behavior is performed with frequency. Indicating dates is helpful.

Decide when to observe. Observe during a time students are normally using books, when they first come into the room in the morning, or during a time they are involved in various learning centers. You may need to initiate the experience with students who do not independently go to books. Collect pertinent data, including written work samples and recordings of oral reading, and keep anecdotal records. Speak with parents for additional input.

ASSESSMENT
RUNNING RECORDS

An effective reader uses the visual information, based on knowledge of language and the content, to predict what comes next in the text, to check this prediction by taking in new visual information or by thinking about whether the prediction makes sense, and to confirm or reject this prediction in the light of this new information. If the prediction is rejected, the reader self-corrects.

When a student reads aloud, you can record what is read and look more closely at what the student is thinking and doing. Oral reading miscues reveal a student's reading strategies. Any miscues can be analyzed to make teaching decisions about the suitability of the level of the guided reading books being read and about the type of help a student may need. One way of doing this is to take a running record of oral reading.

Using a Running Record
Follow this assessment procedure to periodically monitor reading strategies.

First Step	Select something that is known to the student for him or her to read orally. (If it is too familiar, the reading may not reveal much information about the child's thinking.) This may be: • **a guided reading book** • **a poem** • **a dictated piece of the student's writing** • **some of the student's published personal writing**
Second Step	Ask the student to read the selected piece aloud. Record the student's reading in one of these ways: • **Record the correct reading and miscues on a blank piece of paper as the student reads, keeping the same linear arrangement of the text.** OR • **Make a copy of the text and mark the miscues on it as the student reads.**
Third Step	Tabulate the miscues. Use symbols to indicate what the student is doing. Some usual conventions follow.

Accurate reading	✓✓✓	(checks follow test pattern)
Substitution	wet (*child*)	
	Went (*text*)	
Attempt	w-we-wet	
	went	
Self-correction	wet	
	Went SC	
Omission	-	(or circle word)
	went	
Insertion	is	(or use carat)
	went	
Teacher told	-	(or underline word)
	Went T	
Repetition (of word or sentence)	R2 (numeral indicates number of repeats)	(or wavy underlines)

Evaluation: Analysis of the Running Record

Miscues in oral reading performance help you to identify the strategies a student uses. Ask yourself why the student makes each error. To determine what cues the student depends on, consider the following:

- Does the student use visual cues from letters and words, such as they for them?

- Does the student use context clues to construct meaning? Inaccurate reading that makes sense indicates the student is probably using prior knowledge or familiar oral language.

- Does the student use knowledge of the grammatical structure of language? Again, the student's own oral language may influence a response.

Make your best guess as to what cues the student uses, recording by the miscues *v* for visual cues, *m* for meaning, and *s* for structure. One or more types of cues might be used for any miscue. By analyzing each miscue in this way you can get an indication of the strategies the student is using, as well as those not being used or those being overused. Also notice instances of self-correction. Self-correction is an important skill in good reading.

Finally, make any notes on the running record about behaviors during the session. All of this information will assist you in assessing the student.

Running Records as a Regular Monitoring Tool

For each student who is able to read some type of continuous text, it is useful to take a running record about every six weeks. Repeat more often for students for whom you have concerns. For fluent readers it would only be necessary at the beginning, middle, and end of the school year.

Establish a system. For example, you might choose one student per school day, keeping the dated record and analysis in each student's portfolio to monitor the progress during the year. Select a time when you can hear the student read without interruptions, such as when other students are engaged in individual quiet reading.

Sample Running Record

Name: _____ Date: _____

Title: _____

PAGE	TEXT INFORMATION USED	RUNNING RECORD	
4	The animals had a picnic	✓ ✓ have ✓ ✓	v, m
	To celebrate the fair.	✓ ✓ ✓ ✓	
	They all brought something tasty	✓ ✓ bought ✓ t/testy/SC	v, m, s
	For everyone to share.	✓ ✓ ✓ ✓	
7	The lambs brought yams.	✓ ✓ bought ✓	v, m, s
	The bees brought peas.	✓ ✓ bought ✓	v, m, s
	The poodles brought noodles	✓ ✓ bought ✓	v, m, s
	All sprinkled with cheese.	✓ sprin/sprinkle/SC ✓	
8	The cheetahs brought pitas.	✓ ✓ bought pasta/T	v, m, s
	The mice brought rice.	✓ ✓ bought ✓	v, m, s
	The moose brought juice	✓ ✓ bought ✓	v, m, s
	And a bucket of ice.	✓ ✓ ✓ ✓ ✓	
11	The pigs brought figs.	✓ ✓ bought ✓	v, m, s
	The bears brought pears.	✓ ✓ bought ✓	v, m, s
	The apes brought grapes	✓ ✓ bought ✓	v, m, s
	And some picnic chairs.	✓ ✓ ✓ ✓	
12	The raccoons brought spoons.	✓ ✓ ✓ ✓	
	The moles brought bowls.	✓ ✓ ✓ ✓	
	The storks brought forks	✓ ✓ ✓ fo/fork/SC	
	And some cinnamon rolls.	✓ ✓ c/cam/camon/T	v
15	The snakes brought cakes	✓ snake bought ✓	v, m, s
	And I brought the tea.	✓ ✓ ✓ ✓ ✓	
	It was a wild picnic –	✓ ✓ ✓ ✓ ✓	
	Just the animals and me!	✓ ✓ ✓ ✓ ✓	

v=visual, m=meaning, s=structure

Calculations

Note: In the example the student repeatedly misread the word *brought* as *bought*. There are two approaches to counting this error: as one error that is repeated or as multiple errors (which the student failed to self-correct).

- **Calculation of Accuracy Rate**

  If *bought* is counted as only one error, accuracy rate is calculated as follows:

  102—(5/102 x 100)=95%

  If *bought* is counted as an error each time it is misread, the accuracy rate is calculated as follows:

  102—(15/102 x 100)=85%

  The calculation of the accuracy rate is expressed by the following generic formula:

  T—(E/T x 100)=AR

- **Calculation of Self-Correction Rate**

  If *bought* is counted as only one error, self-correction rate is (5+3)/3=2.6

  If *bought* is counted as an error each time it is misread, self-correction rate is (15+3)/3=6

  The calculation of the self-correction rate can be expressed by the following formula:

  (E+SC)/SC=SCR

  T=total number of words   E=number of errors
  AR=accuracy rate   SC=number of self-corrections
  SCR=self-correction rate

Teacher's Notes

Adib told the story (pointing to picture) and answered questions. Adib is using all strategies when reading and seems to have cross-checked one cue against another to self-correct. I could draw his attention to the difference between brought *and* bought. *This book is at a suitable level of difficulty for instruction.*

Note that space has also been provided for you to ask your own comprehension questions and record children's responses.

Evaluation of Suitability of Books

If a student is reading at an appropriate instructional level, approximately 94% of the text should be read accurately. An attempt at a word that is eventually correct is not an error; record this as a self-correction and tally it as accurately read. By calculating the percentage of accurately read words and analyzing the types of errors, you'll be able to determine whether the student is reading books at the appropriate instructional level, and you'll be able to choose the right guided reading books for individuals and groups.

Students may select a guided reading book to have it read to them or to read with a partner. In these instances the book may be easier or harder than the instructional level.

RUNNING RECORD
BENCHMARK BOOK LEVEL A

Running Record Sheet
Fruit Salad

Name _____   Date _____

22 Words   Level A   Accuracy Rate _____

PAGE	TEXT	RUNNING RECORD ANALYSIS
Page 2	We have apples.	
Page 3	We have oranges.	
Page 4	We have bananas.	
Page 5	We have berries.	
Page 6	We have melons.	
Page 7	We have grapes.	
Page 8	We have fruit salad!	

Comprehension:

1) _____

_____

_____

_____

2) _____

_____

_____

_____

RUNNING RECORD
BENCHMARK BOOK LEVEL B

Running Record Sheet
Puppy Paints

Name _____   Date _____

28 Words   Level B   Accuracy Rate _____

PAGE	TEXT	RUNNING RECORD ANALYSIS
Page 2	Puppy sees a flower.	
Page 3	Puppy paints a flower.	
Page 4	Puppy sees a doll.	
Page 5	Puppy paints a doll.	
Page 6	Puppy sees a cat.	
Page 7	Puppy paints a cat.	
Page 8	Puppy likes his paintings!	

Comprehension:

1) _____

_____

_____

_____

2) _____

_____

_____

_____

RUNNING RECORD
BENCHMARK BOOK LEVEL C

Running Record Sheet
Ready Freddy

Name _____   Date _____

49 Words   Level C   Accuracy Rate _____

PAGE	TEXT	RUNNING RECORD ANALYSIS
Page 2	Freddy gets ready. Freddy puts on his red jacket.	
Page 3	Freddy puts on his blue snow pants.	
Page 4	Freddy puts on his yellow boots.	
Page 5	Freddy puts on his green hat.	
Page 6	Freddy puts on his orange mittens.	
Page 7	Freddy gets Skip. Is Freddy ready?	
Page 8	Yes! Freddy is ready to play in the snow.	

Comprehension:

1) _____

_____

_____

_____

2) _____

_____

_____

_____

RUNNING RECORD
BENCHMARK BOOK LEVEL D

Running Record Sheet
Ice Cream

Name _____   Date _____

58 Words   Level D   Accuracy Rate _____

PAGE	TEXT	RUNNING RECORD ANALYSIS
Page 2	Rabbit wanted ice cream. Rabbit said, "One scoop, please."	
Page 3	And Little Bird said, "I'll have one scoop, please."	
Page 4	Fox wanted ice cream. Fox said, "Two scoops, please."	
Page 5	And Little Mouse said, "I'll have two scoops, please."	
Page 6	Moose wanted ice cream. Moose said, "Ten scoops, please."	
Page 7	And Little Frog said, "TEN SCOOPS? That's too much! You will get sick!"	

Comprehension:

1) _____

_____

_____

_____

_____

_____

2) _____

_____

_____

_____

_____

RUNNING RECORD
BENCHMARK BOOK LEVEL E

Running Record Sheet
Ring! Ring!

Name _____ Date _____

109 Words   Level E   Accuracy Rate _____

PAGE	TEXT	RUNNING RECORD ANALYSIS
Page 2	RING! RING! RING! RING! The phone rang.	
Page 4	Rose was playing ball in the yard. "I'll get the phone. I think it's for me!" Rose said.	
Page 6	Rex was flying a kite in the yard. "I'll get the phone," Rex said. "I think it's for me!"	
Page 8	Mom was washing the dog. "I'll get the phone!" Mom said. "I think it's for me!"	
Page 10	Dad was washing the car. Dad said, "I'll get the phone! I think it's for me!"	
Page 12	RING! RING! RING! RING! Rose ran to get the phone. Rex ran to get the phone. Dad ran to get the phone. Mom ran to get the phone. But Skippy got there first.	
Page 14	RING! RING! RING! RING! Skippy ran out to the yard.	

Comprehension:

1) _____

_____

2) _____

_____

TM ® & © Scholastic Inc. *Ring! Ring!* by Janelle Cherrington. Copyright © 2011 by Scholastic Inc. Published by Scholastic Inc.

RUNNING RECORD
BENCHMARK BOOK LEVEL F

Running Record Sheet
Little Bird

Name _____   Date _____

114 Words   Level F   Accuracy Rate _____

PAGE	TEXT	RUNNING RECORD ANALYSIS
Page 2	Little Bird came out of her nest. She flapped her wings. And then ... she jumped!	
Page 4	Little Bird flapped and flapped her wings. Little Bird was flying!	
Page 6	Up and up Little Bird flew! She flew away from her nest. She flew and flew.	
Page 7	She flew far.	
Page 8	Little Bird flew to a berry tree. She ate a red berry. Yum!	
Page 10	Little Bird flew to a puddle. She drank from the cool blue puddle. Yum!	
Page 12	It was time to go home. Little Bird flew and flew. But she did not see her tree. Little Bird was lost. "Can you help me find my nest?" said Little Bird. "Come with me. I will help you," said the fox.	

Comprehension:

1) _____

_____

2) _____

_____

TM ® & © Scholastic Inc. *Little Bird* by Libby Brereton. Copyright © 2011 by Scholastic Inc. Published by Scholastic Inc.

RUNNING RECORD
BENCHMARK BOOK LEVEL G

Running Record Sheet
Our Tree House

Name _____   Date _____

110 Words   Level G   Accuracy Rate _____

PAGE	TEXT	RUNNING RECORD ANALYSIS
Page 2	Squirrel, Raccoon, and Bird had a tree house. The tree house had a big room. It had a trap door. It was the best tree house in town.	
Page 3	Squirrel, Raccoon, and Bird were in a club. They had meetings in their tree house.	
Page 4	Cat, Mouse, and Hamster did not have a tree house. They were not in the club.	
Page 5	One day, Cat went up a tree. He looked in the tree house. He saw the big room. He saw the trap door. It was the best tree house in town.	
Page 6	"Mouse! Hamster! Come and see," said Cat. Mouse and Hamster went up to see. "Let's play up here," said Mouse.	

Comprehension:

1) _____

_____

_____

2) _____

_____

_____

RUNNING RECORD
BENCHMARK BOOK LEVEL H

Running Record Sheet
The Story of Henny Penny

Name _____   Date _____

115 Words   Level H   Accuracy Rate _____

PAGE	TEXT	RUNNING RECORD ANALYSIS
Page 2	Henny Penny was under the oak tree. She was eating her corn.	
Page 3	Something fell. It hit Henny Penny on her head. "Ouch!" said Henny Penny.	
Page 4	Henny Penny looked up at the sky. Then Henny Penny cried, "The sky is falling! The sky is falling! I must go and tell the king!"	
Page 6	Soon, Henny Penny met a duck. "The sky is falling! The sky is falling! I must go and tell the king!" said Henny Penny.	
Page 7	"May I go with you?" asked the duck. "Yes, you can!" said Henny Penny.	
Page 8	Soon Henny Penny and the duck met a goose. "The sky is falling! The sky is falling! I must go and tell the king!" said Henny Penny.	

Comprehension:

1) _____

_____

_____

2) _____

_____

_____

RUNNING RECORD
BENCHMARK BOOK LEVEL I

Running Record Sheet
Hi! Fly Guy

Name _____   Date _____

101 Words   Level I   Accuracy Rate _____

PAGE	TEXT	RUNNING RECORD ANALYSIS
Page 10	Buzz took the fly home. "This is my pet," Buzz said to Mom and Dad.	
Page 11	"He is smart. He can say my name. Listen!" Buzz opened the jar. The fly flew out.	
Page 12	"Flies can't be pets!" said Dad. "They are pests!" He got the fly swatter. The fly cried—BUZZ!	
Page 13	And Buzz came to the rescue. "You are right," said Dad. "This fly is smart!"	
Page 14	"He needs a name," said Mom. Buzz thought for a minute. "Fly Guy," said Buzz. And Fly Guy said—BUZZ!	
Page 15	It was time for lunch. Buzz gave Fly Guy something to eat.	
Page 16	Fly Guy was happy.	

Comprehension:

1) _____

_____

_____

2) _____

_____

_____

RUNNING RECORD
BENCHMARK BOOK LEVEL J

Running Record Sheet
The Rain Came Down

Name _____   Date _____

109 Words   Level J   Accuracy Rate _____

PAGE	TEXT	RUNNING RECORD ANALYSIS
Page 3	On Saturday morning, the rain came down. It made the chickens squawk.	
Page 4	The cat yowled at the chickens, and the dog barked at the cat.	
Page 5	And still, the rain came down.	
Page 6	The man yelled at the dog and woke up the baby. "Stop all that yelling!" shouted the man's wife.	
Page 7	The dog barked louder. And still, the rain came down.	
Page 8	A policeman heard the noise and stopped to see what was wrong.	
Page 9	His car was blocking traffic, and half a block away, a woman squirmed in the back of a taxi.	
Page 10	"Hurry up, or I'll miss my plane!" she told the taxi driver. So he started honking his horn.	

Comprehension:

1) _____

_____

_____

2) _____

_____

_____

RUNNING RECORD
BENCHMARK BOOK LEVEL K

Running Record Sheet
Frog and Toad All Year

Name _____   Date _____

114 Words   Level K   Accuracy Rate _____

PAGE	TEXT	RUNNING RECORD ANALYSIS
Page 4	Frog knocked at Toad's door. "Toad, wake up," he cried. "Come out and see how wonderful the winter is!" "I will not," said Toad. "I am in my warm bed." "Winter is beautiful," said Frog "Come out and have fun."	
Page 5	"Blah," said Toad. "I do not have any winter clothes."	
Page 6	Frog came into the house. "I have brought you some things to wear," he said. Frog pushed a coat down over the top of Toad. Frog pulled snowpants up over the bottom of Toad.	
Page 7	He put a hat and scarf on Toad's head. "Help!" cried Toad. "My best friend is trying to kill me!" "I am only getting you ready for winter," said Frog.	

Comprehension:

1) _____

_____

2) _____

_____

TM ® & © Scholastic Inc. *Frog and Toad All Year* by Arnold Lobel. Copyright © 1976 by Arnold Lobel. Published by Scholastic Inc. by arrangement with HarperCollins Publishers.

GUIDED READING Text Types

Running Record Sheet
The Subway Mouse

Name _____   Date _____

91 Words   Level L   Accuracy Rate _____

PAGE	TEXT	RUNNING RECORD ANALYSIS
Page 6	When he grew big enough to hunt for food, Nib explored the station floor. He found strange things, beautiful things, and things that reminded him of his favorite stories. He started to bring these things home.	
Page 7	"Your garbage is crowding our babies!" the mothers complained. "Your babies are nibbling my stuff!" Nib answered. Then he had an idea.	
Page 8	He found an empty corner and built a snug hideout. Nib loved to come home, wash up, and fall asleep surrounded by his colorful treasures.	
Page 9	He traveled to Tunnel's End in his dreams.	

Comprehension:

1) _____

_____

_____

_____

2) _____

_____

_____

_____

_____

RUNNING RECORD
BENCHMARK BOOK LEVEL M

Running Record Sheet
Flat Stanley

Name _____   Date _____

132 Words   Level M   Accuracy Rate _____

PAGE	TEXT	RUNNING RECORD ANALYSIS
Page 8	Being flat could be fun. Stanley enjoyed going in and out of rooms by sliding through the crack at the bottom of the door. Arthur tried too, but he just banged his head. Being flat could be exciting. During the holidays, Stanley was invited to visit his friend Thomas in California. Mr. Lambchop brought home an enormous brown paper envelope and said, "Stanley, try this on for size." The envelope fit Stanley perfectly, and the next morning his parents slid him into it, along with an egg-salad sandwich, and mailed him from a box on the corner.	
Page 10	Stanley had a fine time in California.	
Page 11	Thomas's family returned him in a beautiful white envelope they had made themselves. They marked it AIRMAIL and wrote VALUABLE and THIS END UP on both sides.	

Comprehension:

1) _____

_____

_____

2) _____

_____

_____

RUNNING RECORD
BENCHMARK BOOK LEVEL N

Running Record Sheet
Brand-new School, Brave New Ruby (Ruby and the Booker Boys)

Name _____   Date _____

116 Words   Level N   Accuracy Rate _____

PAGE	TEXT	RUNNING RECORD ANALYSIS
Page 29	We were a block away from the school. I could see everybody standing outside on the blacktop. It looked like a parade of kids. Not a little parade, but the big Thanksgiving Day parade they have in New York City. My old school only went up to the fifth grade. Hope Road Academy started at kindergarten and went all the way up to the eighth grade. That means a lot more kids. I looked all over for my friend Teresa, but I didn't see her anywhere.	
Page 30	I started to get really extra-crazy nervous then. I didn't know anyone except for my brothers. Marcellus must have seen the scared look on my face. He put his arm around my shoulders.	

Comprehension:

1) _____

_____

_____

_____

2) _____

_____

_____

_____

RUNNING RECORD
BENCHMARK BOOK LEVEL O

Running Record Sheet
John Philip Duck

Name _____   Date _____

127 Words   Level O   Accuracy Rate _____

PAGE	TEXT	RUNNING RECORD ANALYSIS
Page 25	Edward turned on the music. It was a Sousa march, and John Philip was in the best form he had ever been. He did all of his tricks without a hitch. He marched to and from the fountain. He hopped in and out of the fountain pool on command, just as Edward had taught him. When John Philip was done, he waddled up to Mr. Schutt and cocked his head. "Well, I never did see!" Mr. Schutt said almost in a whisper. One of the hotel guests had seen it all and commented to Mr. Schutt, "What an unusual touch." A well-dressed lady cooed, "I've never seen, in all of my world of travel, a hotel with live ducks swimming in the lobby fountain! Wonderful, simply wonderful!"	

Comprehension:

1) _____

_____

_____

_____

2) _____

_____

_____

_____

RUNNING RECORD
BENCHMARK BOOK LEVEL P

TM ® & © Scholastic Inc. *97 Ways to Train a Dragon (Dragon Slayers' Academy #9)* by Kate McMullan. Text copyright © 2003 by Kate McMullan. Published by Scholastic Inc. by arrangement with Penguin Group (USA) Inc.

Running Record Sheet
97 Ways to Train a Dragon (Dragon Slayers' Academy)

Name _____   Date _____

135 Words   Level P   Accuracy Rate _____

PAGE	TEXT	RUNNING RECORD ANALYSIS
Page 21	By the time the boys ran into the dining hall, it was empty. "You've missed breakfast," said Frypot the cook. "Lucky for you I've still got some eel-meal." He handed them steaming bowls of hot cereal. Wiglaf stared at the quivering gray lump. Even Angus turned up his nose. "Is there nothing else?" In the end, they choked it down. Then they went off to scrub alongside their classmates. As he scrubbed, Wiglaf thought about the purple egg. He wondered what the little pipling inside might look like. Would it peep? Would it have tiny wings?	
Page 22	By the time Angus and Wiglaf and some other boys staggered back to the dorm room that night, they were too tired to think. Angus threw himself fully dressed onto his cot. Two seconds later, he was snoring.	

Comprehension:

1) _____

 _____

2) _____

 _____

RUNNING RECORD
BENCHMARK BOOK LEVEL Q

Running Record Sheet
Nothing Ever Happens on 90th Street

Name _____   Date _____

145 Words   Level Q   Accuracy Rate _____

PAGE	TEXT	RUNNING RECORD ANALYSIS
Page 9	"Writing?" Alexis Leora asked Eva. "Yes," Eva answered. Alexis Leora did six deep knee bends and then sighed. "Stretch," she said sadly. "Use your imagination. If your story doesn't go the way you want it to, you can always stretch the truth. You can ask, 'What if?' and make up a better story." "You're right," Eva said, thinking "What if?" What if Alexis Leora met someone? Would she smile then? What would that look like? Eva closed her eyes to try to picture it, but all she could picture was soup—Spanish soup—rich and brown and so spicy it seemed as if she could actually smell it.	
Page 10	She could! When Eva opened her eyes, Mrs. Martinez was standing beside her. She nodded to Alexis Leora as she handed Eva a bowl of soup. "Have some," she said. "Writers *need* soup. What's your story about?"	

Comprehension:

1) _____

   _____

   _____

2) _____

   _____

   _____

   _____

RUNNING RECORD
BENCHMARK BOOK LEVEL R

Running Record Sheet
Miracles on Maple Hill

Name _____   Date _____

161 Words   Level R   Accuracy Rate _____

PAGE	TEXT	RUNNING RECORD ANALYSIS
Page 35	Marly stood by the side of the huge pans. You could look forever and forever into the bubbling, deeper and deeper, but your looking was always coming up again. She tried watching one bubble, all by itself, but she couldn't. It was gone, and another one was in its place too quickly. It was like ten thousand pots of taffy boiling all at once. The sap in the pans at the back looked like water, just as it did in the buckets on the trees, but each pan nearer the front was	
Page 36	more and more golden, because each one was closer to being real syrup. Mr. Chris said he had to boil away *forty* gallons of sap to make *one* little gallon of syrup. "How many gallons will one tree give?" Daddy asked, and Marly knew why he wanted to know. On Maple Hill there were about fifty maple trees. She could practically see Daddy's arithmetic getting ready to start working.	

Comprehension:

1) _____

_____

_____

2) _____

_____

_____

RUNNING RECORD
BENCHMARK BOOK LEVEL S

Running Record Sheet
The Good Dog

Name _____   Date _____

119 Words   Level S   Accuracy Rate _____

PAGE	TEXT	RUNNING RECORD ANALYSIS
Page 195	They pushed on, traveling slowly but steadily. Suddenly, McKinley stopped. He lifted his nose and sniffed. A low growl rose in his chest.	
Page 196	Aspen drew close. "What is it?" McKinley cocked his head and flicked his ears forward. "I'm not sure." Lupin snapped, "Humans?" Her eyes were half lidded with encrusted snow. McKinley sighed. "I think so. They're off that way." He pointed his nose to show her. "If we keep following the creek, we'll be heading right toward them. We have to go a different way." "But if we leave the water," Lupin whined, "won't it be easier for that dog to follow us?" Aspen stepped forward. "Lupin, I think McKinley is saying we don't have a choice."	

Comprehension:

1) _____

_____

_____

_____

2) _____

_____

_____

_____

RUNNING RECORD
BENCHMARK BOOK LEVEL T

Running Record Sheet
The Word Eater

Name _____   Date _____

156 Words   Level T   Accuracy Rate _____

PAGE	TEXT	RUNNING RECORD ANALYSIS
Page 23	Out of nowhere, a huge crow flew toward Lerner's window. Lerner ducked instinctively, but the crow didn't thump against the glass as she'd expected. Instead, it landed awkwardly on the ledge, gobbled something in its beak, and flew away. Bobby laughed at Lerner's response. "Did you think it was going to fly in and eat you, Helmet Head?" As usual, Lerner ignored him. The window was an ancient kind that pushed open from the bottom, and it was open a crack. Lerner reached over to close it and noticed a tiny movement on the white concrete ledge. A bug? A caterpillar? She opened the window more and leaned out for a closer look. A rosy worm, about the length of two rice grains, wriggled toward the window as if trying to find a place to hide. Lerner wasn't crazy about worms, but she didn't like the thought of him being gobbled up by some obnoxious crow.	

Comprehension:

1) _____

_____

_____

2) _____

_____

_____

RUNNING RECORD
BENCHMARK BOOK LEVEL U

Running Record Sheet
My Side of the Mountain

Name _____   Date _____

135 Words   Level U   Accuracy Rate _____

PAGE	TEXT	RUNNING RECORD ANALYSIS
Page 13	I looked into the stream to see what else I could eat, and as I did, my hand knocked a rotten log apart. I remembered about old logs and all the sleeping stages of insects that are in it. I chopped away until I found a cold white grub. I swiftly tied a string to my hook, put the grub on, and walked up the stream looking for a good place to fish. All the manuals I had read were very emphatic about where fish lived, and so I had memorized this: "In streams, fish usually congregate in pools and deep calm water. The heads of riffles, small rapids, the tail of a pool, eddies below rocks or logs, deep undercut banks, in the shade of overhanging bushes—all are very likely places to fish."	

Comprehension:

1) _____

_____

_____

_____

2) _____

_____

_____

_____

TM ® & © Scholastic Inc. *My Side of the Mountain* by Jean Craighead George. Copyright © 1959, 1988 by Jean Craighead George. Published by Scholastic Inc. by arrangement with Penguin Group (USA) Inc.

RUNNING RECORD
BENCHMARK BOOK LEVEL V

Running Record Sheet
Black Star, Bright Dawn

Name _____   Date _____

159 Words   Level V   Accuracy Rate _____

PAGE	TEXT	RUNNING RECORD ANALYSIS
Page 63	"One day the Great Spirit visited the earth to look at the creatures he had created. Walking through a village at evening time, he heard people singing the sunset song. The trees were filled with birds of every color, but none of them were singing. All were silent, listening to the sunset song.	
Page 64	"'Why do the birds not sing?' the Great Spirit asked. "'Because they have no voices,' the people said. "'What a terrible mistake,' the Great Spirit said. "At once he called all the birds together. Hundreds, thousands of them came from everywhere. They darkened the sky. They made thunder with their beating wings. "'At dawn,' he said to them, 'you are to fly as high as you can. When you reach the limits of your strength, then you will find your voice. The bird who flies the highest will find the most beautiful voice in the world and return to earth to sing the most beautiful songs.'"	

Comprehension:

1) _____

_____

_____

2) _____

_____

_____

TM ® & © Scholastic Inc. *Black Star, Bright Dawn* by Scott O'Dell. Copyright © 1998 by Scott O'Dell. Published by Scholastic Inc. by arrangement with Houghton Mifflin Harcourt Publishing Company.

RUNNING RECORD
BENCHMARK BOOK LEVEL W

Running Record Sheet
The Titan's Curse (Percy Jackson & the Olympians)

Name _____   Date _____

142 Words   Level W   Accuracy Rate _____

PAGE	TEXT	RUNNING RECORD ANALYSIS
Page 45	Finally the sky began to lighten. Artemis muttered, "About time. He's so-o-o lazy during the winter." "You're, um, waiting for sunrise?" I asked. "For my brother. Yes." I didn't want to be rude. I mean, I knew the legends about Apollo—or sometimes Helios—driving a big sun chariot across the sky. But I also knew that the sun was really a star about a zillion miles away. I'd gotten used to some of the Greek myths being true, but still. . . I didn't see how Apollo could drive the sun. "It's not exactly as you think," Artemis said, like she was reading my mind. "Oh, okay." I started to relax. "So, it's not like he'll be pulling up in a—" There was a sudden burst of light on the horizon. A blast of warmth. "Don't look," Artemis advised. "Not until he parks."	

Comprehension:

1) _____

_____

_____

2) _____

_____

_____

RUNNING RECORD
BENCHMARK BOOK LEVEL X

Running Record Sheet
The Mostly True Adventures of Homer P. Figg

Name _____   Date _____

142 Words   Level X   Accuracy Rate _____

PAGE	TEXT	RUNNING RECORD ANALYSIS
Page 88	After a while Mr. Willow's voice kind of blends into the sound of the wheels clicking against the rails. It's amazing what goes by the windows on a train. Farms and fields and forests, and rows of wooden houses, and big brick mills. Like we're floating through a storybook and each turn in the track is a new page, and it's a story I never heard before so I don't know how it will end. Page after page, picture after picture, and always something new around the corner, and the chugging of the locomotive belching black smoke, making its own dark clouds against the sky, and the steam whistle sounding alive somehow, like the whole train is saying *Here-I-am, make-way-chugga-chugga-woowoo! Here-I-am, make-way-chugga-chugga-woowoo!* and rocking me to sleep. When I wake up we're in Portland, and that's where the trouble really starts.	

Comprehension:

1) _____

_____

_____

2) _____

_____

_____

RUNNING RECORD
BENCHMARK BOOK LEVEL Y

Running Record Sheet
The Devil's Arithmetic

Name _____   Date _____

167 Words   Level Y   Accuracy Rate _____

PAGE	TEXT	RUNNING RECORD ANALYSIS
Page 57	The forest was now boiling with people, for the Viosk villagers had come behind the *klezmer* to greet Shmuel and his friends. Hannah hung back. More people meant more greetings and more excuses. It was worse than a family party at home. *At home!* The skin on her face suddenly felt stretched tight across her cheekbones and her eyes began to prickle with tears. *Where was her home?* She forced herself to recall the house in New Rochelle with its borders of flowers and the flagstone walk. But the image seemed to be fading, especially when compared with the forest full of villagers and the tiny house and the horse barn she'd left just hours before. A hand on her arm riveted her to the moment. "Come, Chaya," Gitl said. "Come and meet your new aunt-to-be." Pulling Hannah past the noisy celebrants, Gitl led her to the one wagon facing the rest, where the men were busy at work encouraging the two strong workhorses to turn around.	

Comprehension:

1) _____

_____

2) _____

_____

TM ® & © Scholastic Inc. *The Devil's Arithmetic* by Jane Yolen. Copyright © 1988 by Jane Yolen. Published by Scholastic Inc. by arrangement with Penguin Group (USA) Inc.

Running Record Sheet
The Hunger Games

Name _____   Date _____

186 Words   Level Z   Accuracy Rate _____

PAGE	TEXT	RUNNING RECORD ANALYSIS
Page 239	Soon the seal's in the sky, the anthem plays in my right ear. I see the boy from District 1, Rue. That's all for tonight. *Six of us left*, I think. *Only six.* With the bread still locked in my hands, I fall asleep at once. Sometimes when things are particularly bad, my brain will give me a happy dream. I visit with my father in the woods. An hour of sunlight and cake with Prim. Tonight it sends me Rue, still decked in her flowers, perched in a high sea of trees, trying to teach me to talk to the mockingjays. I see no sign of her wounds, no blood, just a bright, laughing	
Page 240	girl. She sings songs I've never heard in a clear, melodic voice. On and on. Through the night. There's a drowsy in-between period when I can hear the last few strains of her music although she's lost in the leaves. When I fully awaken, I'm momentarily comforted. I try to hold on to the peaceful feeling of the dream, but it quickly slips away, leaving me sadder and lonelier than ever.	

Comprehension:

1) _____

_____

2) _____

_____

GUIDELINES FOR **ASSESSING** READING COMPREHENSION THROUGH **RETELLING**

Select similar texts.	When comparing a student's retelling over time, use the same type of text each time. Compare narratives with other narratives and nonfiction texts with other nonfiction texts. Also select similar levels unless you are purposely moving a struggling reader down a level to discover an independent reading level or moving a reader up to a more challenging level.
Prepare a guide sheet.	In preparation for retelling, preview a text to determine what kinds of ideas and information you will be listening for in the student retelling. You may want to create a guide sheet or checklist that you can refer to and use for taking notes.

For fiction texts, include on your checklist:

- **title and author name**
- **genre**
- **character names and a note whether they are major or minor characters**
- **note about the setting, including any changes in setting**
- **brief description of the problem, conflict, or goal in the story**
- **list of important events in sequential order in the beginning, middle, and end**
- **brief description of how the problem or conflict is solved, or the goal reached**

For nonfiction texts, include on your checklist:

- **title and author name**
- **genre**
- **book topic**
- **main idea of the book and of any sections or chapters**
- **important details that support main ideas**
- **important people included if the book is a narrative**
- **important events listed in sequential order**
- **text features such as photographs or illustrations, diagrams, charts, and maps**

Ask the student to retell the text.	Make sure the student has recently read the text selected for the retelling. Then ask the student to retell the story or information, starting at the beginning and telling what happened or what the author said about the topic. As the student retells, make checks or notes on your guide sheet that will help you recall what the student included and the sequence of information. If you find it difficult to make checks or notes, it may be because the student is retelling information out of sequential order, has omitted important ideas, is focusing on unimportant information, or has not comprehended the main idea or the plot. For events or information told out of sequence, you may want to number the order of ideas students express instead of just checking them off.

Listen for what the student says and does not say.

When you listen to a retelling, listen for what the student says and how the student retells a fiction or nonfiction text. What the student leaves out is as important as what he or she says as an indicator of comprehension and understanding.

In a fiction retelling, listen for:

- **characters' names**
- **important events in sequence**
- **important details**
- **use of language and vocabulary from the story**
- **understanding of how the story is organized**
- **understanding of the genre, such as whether a student knows a story is realistic, a fantasy, or a special type of literature such as a folktale, fable, or mystery, as evidenced by mention of setting, understanding that characters are imaginary, connection with realistic situations and people, or a description of clues that lead to solving a mystery**

In a nonfiction retelling, listen for:

- **statement of what the text is about**
- **statements of main ideas**
- **key ideas and facts**
- **mention of text features from which the student derived information, such as a photograph or illustration, chart, diagram, or map**
- **use of language and vocabulary from the text**
- **understanding of the genre, such as whether the student points out that the text describes or explains a topic, tells about the life of a person or is told by that person, or narrates an important time or event in history**
- **understanding of how the text is organized by mention of details that support main ideas, or how the author explained or described a topic, presented a problem and solution, showed causes and effects, or compared and contrasted people, things, or ideas**

Provide prompts if needed.

When a student is retelling, let him finish without prompting for information. If the retelling is incomplete, out of order, or leaves out important information, you may want to prompt with more specific questions about parts of the text the student misunderstood or did not include. Note how many prompts are needed to complete the retelling.

Summarize and evaluate the retelling.

Using your guide sheet, discuss and review the retelling with the student to help her understand what can be improved and how. This process also helps you develop instructional goals for future sessions.

You can also use your guide sheet to help you evaluate the retelling at a later time and determine what level the student is on and what instruction she needs. Keep your guide sheets for each student retelling to give you information for determining student progress and points for intervention.

Evaluating Students' Retellings

Students' retellings of fiction and nonfiction will give you a snapshot of where students fall in their ability to process and comprehend text. The following criteria for establishing levels can aid you in placing a student at a particular level and help you plan for instruction.

FICTION

Level	Criteria for Establishing Level
3	Most-complete retellings: • **Indicate an understanding of the genre through description of and connections made to setting, characters, and plot** • **Present a sequence of actions and events** • **Provide explanations for the motivations behind characters' actions** • **Include character names** • **Elaborate using important details from the story** • **Comment on or evaluate the story** • **Do not require prompts during retelling**
2	Less complex retellings: • **Indicate a basic understanding of genre in brief comments of characters, setting, and plot** • **Present concrete events in sequence** • **Supply missing information through appropriate inferences** • **Include some explanation of the causes of events or characters' motivations** • **Include some important details** • **Require one or two prompts during retelling**
1	Simple descriptive retellings: • **Are partial or limited** • **Indicate a lack of awareness of genre through no mention of a genre's features** • **Have simple beginning, middle, and end** • **May include events out of sequence** • **May describe a setting** • **Present an initiating event and the outcome of a problem** • **Include misinterpretations** • **Refer to characters as "he" or "she" rather than by name** • **Require three or more prompts during retelling**

NONFICTION

Level	Criteria for Establishing Level
3	Most-complete retellings: • **Show a comprehension of the topic** • **Indicate an understanding of the genre in a description of the text, its purpose, and how it is organized** • **Present main ideas of whole text and parts of text** • **Provide important details that support main ideas** • **Include key ideas and facts** • **Elaborate using details enhanced by prior knowledge** • **Comment on or evaluate the text** • **Do not require prompts during retelling**
2	Less complex retellings: • **Show a basic comprehension of the topic** • **Indicate a basic understanding of the genre and text organization in a description of the book** • **Present concrete related facts or events in sequence** • **Supply missing information through appropriate inferences** • **Include some main ideas** • **Provide some important details that support main ideas** • **Mention some key ideas and facts, but omit others** • **Require one or two prompts during retelling**
1	Simple descriptive retellings: • **Are partial or limited** • **Provide the topic of the text** • **Include misinterpretations** • **Include general ideas without focusing on specific main ideas** • **Omit important details to support main ideas** • **Do not include comments on text structure** • **Require three or more prompts during retelling**

BENCHMARK BOOKS

Level	Benchmark Book
Level A	Fruit Salad
Level B	Puppy Paints
Level C	Ready Freddy
Level D	Ice Cream
Level E	My New School
Level F	Small Treasures
Level G	Our Tree House
Level H	Captain Cat
Level I	Hi! Fly Guy
Level J	The Rain Came Down
Level K	Frog and Toad All Year
Level L	The Subway Mouse
Level M	Flat Stanley
Level N	Brand-New School, Brave New Ruby (Ruby and the Booker Boys)
Level O	John Philip Duck
Level P	97 Ways to Train a Dragon (Dragon Slayers' Academy)
Level Q	Nothing Ever Happens on 90th Street
Level R	Miracles on Maple Hill
Level S	The Good Dog
Level T	The Word Eater
Level U	My Side of the Mountain
Level V	Black Star, Bright Dawn
Level W	The Titan's Curse (Percy Jackson & the Olympians)
Level X	The Mostly True Adventures of Homer P. Figg
Level Y	The Devil's Arithmetic
Level Z	The Hunger Games

READING LEVEL CORRELATIONS*

Grade Level (Basal)	Guided Reading Levels	DRA Levels	Success For All Levels	Reading Recovery Levels	Stages of Reading	Lexiles	DRP Text
Kindergarten	A B	A 2	1–3	A–B, 2	Emergent		
Pre-Primer	C D E	3–4 6 8	4–25 25	3–4 5–6 7–8	Emergent/ Early	BR–200	
Primer	F G	10 12	26–27	9–10 12	Early/ Transitional	200–300	
1st Grade	H I	14 16	38–48	14 16	Early/ Transitional	300–400	25–30
2nd Grade	J–K L–M	16–18 20–24	2.0	18 20	Transitional Fluency/ Extending	400–550	30–44
3rd Grade	N O–P	28–30 34–38	3.0	22 24	Fluency/ Extending	600–700	44–54
4th Grade	Q–R	40	4.0	26	Fluency/ Extending Advanced	750–900	46–55
5th Grade	S–V	50	—	26–28	Fluency/ Extending Advanced	850–950	49–57
6th Grade	W–Y Z	60 70–80	—	30 32–34	Advanced	950– 1050	51–60

*See **Text Gradient Chart** on the back of your materials folder. This chart identifies the overlapping level ranges for each grade in the *Scholastic Guided Reading Program.*

USING THE
GUIDED READING PROGRAM

Characteristics of Text

The easiest books are included in Levels A and B. We suggest that children begin using Level A books for guided reading after they have listened to many stories and participated in shared reading. They should have some familiarity with print and understand that you read print and move from left to right in doing so. Children need not know all the letters of the alphabet and their sounds before reading Level A books.

Level A includes picture books without words, some with simple labels or captions, and some with as many as five or six words, often on one line.

In general, these books have clear, easy-to-read print with generous space between words. These simple formats enable young children to focus on print and reading from left to right, while gradually increasing their control over more words. Many of the books have high-frequency words and repeating language patterns. Print is presented in a variety of ways, which helps children become flexible readers from the start. In general, the books focus on topics that are familiar to most children. Books with more complex topics usually have fewer words and will require more of an introduction and teacher-child interaction to support understanding.

Behaviors to Notice and Support

	Child's Name						
Understands familiar concepts in stories and illustrations							
Differentiates print from pictures							
Holds the book and turns pages from right to left							
Reads words from left to right							
Begins to match word by word, pointing with one finger under words							
Locates both known and new words							
Remembers and uses language patterns							
Relates the book to his/her experience							

USING THE
GUIDED READING PROGRAM

Characteristics of Text

Level B books generally have simple story lines or a single idea. The print is easy to read, with adequate space between words so that children can point to words as they read. Books at this level generally have one or two lines of print on a page, somewhat longer sentences, and a variety of punctuation.

There is direct correspondence between the text and pictures, and repeating patterns support the reader. Topics are generally familiar to most children. If more complex concepts are involved, the reading of the book will require teacher-child interaction to support understanding.

Behaviors to Notice and Support

	Child's Name						
Demonstrates control of left-to-right movement and return sweep							
Begins to control word-by-word matching across two lines of text, pointing with one finger							
Notices and interprets detail in pictures							
Talks about ideas in the text							
Remembers and uses language patterns in text							
Uses knowledge of high-frequency words to check on reading							
Uses word-by-word matching to check on reading							
Notices mismatches in meaning or language							
Uses visual information, such as the first letter of the word, to read known and new words							
Pays close attention to print							
Notices features of letters and words							
Begins to self-monitor, noticing mismatches in meaning or language							
Rereads to confirm or figure out new words							

USING THE
GUIDED READING PROGRAM

Characteristics of Text

Level C books have simple story lines and topics that are familiar to most children. Some may offer a new viewpoint on a familiar topic. Level C books generally have more words and lines of print than books at earlier levels. Print is clear and readable, with adequate space between words. Most sentences are simple, but some have more complex structure, offering readers a challenge. While Level C books include some repeating language patterns, these are more complex and there is a shift to more varied patterns. Language patterns are more likely to change from page to page, so children cannot rely on them to make predictions and must pay closer attention to print. Level C books include many high-frequency words, as well as easily decodable words.

Behaviors to Notice and Support

	Child's Name						
Demonstrates control of left-to-right directionality and word-by-word matching across several lines of print							
Begins to track print with eyes							
Rereads to solve problems, such as figuring out new words							
Demonstrates awareness of punctuation by pausing and using some phrasing							
Uses picture details to help figure out words							
Remembers and uses language patterns in text							
Rereads to confirm or figure out new words							
Solves some new words independently							
Controls directionality and word-by-word matching with eyes, using finger at points of difficulty							
Uses visual information to predict, check, and confirm reading							
Recognizes known words quickly and uses them to figure out the meaning of new words							
Searches for understanding while reading							

USING THE
GUIDED READING PROGRAM

Characteristics of Text

Stories at Level D are slightly more complex than at previous levels. Generally, Level D books have topics that are familiar to most children, but also include some abstract or unfamiliar ideas. Text layout is still easy to follow, with both large and small print. Sentences are a little longer than at Level C. Some are carried over to the next page or several pages and use a full range of punctuation. There are more compound words, multisyllabic words, and words with a variety of inflectional endings. Illustrations are still supportive, but less so than at the previous level, requiring the reader to pay more attention to print.

Behaviors to Notice and Support

	Child's Name						
Remembers language patterns and repeating events over longer stretches of text							
Self-corrects, using visual information							
Controls directionality and word-by-word matching with eyes, using finger only at points of difficulty							
Searches for understanding while reading							
Remembers details from the text and pictures							
Pays close attention to words and their structural features (for example, endings)							
Reads fluently, with phrasing							
Rereads to confirm or figure out new words							
Solves new words using knowledge of sound/letter relationships and word parts							

USING THE
GUIDED READING PROGRAM

Characteristics of Text

Level E books are generally longer than books at previous levels, with either more pages or more lines of text on a page. Some have sentences that carry over several pages and have a full range of punctuation. The text structure is generally more complex: stories have more or longer episodes, and informational books have more difficult ideas and concepts. However, in texts with more difficult concepts, there are usually repeating language patterns that offer some support. There are more multisyllabic and compound words at this level.

Behaviors to Notice and Support

	Child's Name							
Tracks print with eyes except at points of difficulty								
Uses language syntax and meaning to read fluently, with phrasing								
Demonstrates awareness of punctuation by pausing, phrasing, and reading with inflection								
Rereads to self-monitor or self-correct phrasing and expression								
Recognizes many words quickly and automatically								
Figures out some longer words by taking them apart								
Relates texts to others previously read								
Reads for meaning but checks with the visual aspects of print (letters, sounds, words)								
Rereads to search for meaning and accuracy								
Remembers details and uses them to clarify meaning								
Demonstrates understanding by talking about text after reading								

USING THE
GUIDED READING PROGRAM

Characteristics of Text

In general, texts at Level F are longer and have more story episodes than at previous levels. There are also shorter texts with some unusual language patterns. Books have some concepts unfamiliar to children and some are even abstract, requiring reflection. Pictures continue to support reading, but closer attention to print is required. Language patterns are more characteristic of written language than of spoken language. Some Level F books have smaller print and more words and lines of text. There are many more new words and a greater variety of high-frequency words. A full range of punctuation is used to enhance meaning.

Behaviors to Notice and Support

	Child's Name							
Tracks print with eyes, using the finger only at points of difficulty								
Demonstrates awareness of punctuation by pausing, phrasing, and reading with inflection								
Uses syntax of written language to figure out new words and their meaning								
Uses sound/letter relationships, word parts, and other visual information to figure out new words								
Uses known words to figure out new words								
Uses multiple sources of information to search and self-correct								
Figures out longer words while reading for meaning								
Rereads to figure out words, self-correct, or improve phrasing and expression								
Rereads to search for meaning								
Recognizes most words quickly and automatically								
Moves quickly through the text								
Reads fluently, with phrasing								
Talks about ideas in the text and relates them to his/her experiences and to other texts								

USING THE
GUIDED READING PROGRAM

Characteristics of Text

Most books at Level G are not repetitive. These books include a variety of patterns. Knowledge of punctuation is important in understanding what the sentence means and how it should be spoken. Vocabulary is more challenging, with a greater range of words and more difficult words, including some that are technical and require content knowledge. Concepts and ideas may be less familiar than at previous levels. Level G books have a greater variety of styles of print and text layout, requiring close attention to print and flexibility on the part of the reader.

Behaviors to Notice and Support

	Child's Name						
Reads fluently and rapidly, with appropriate phrasing							
Follows print with eyes, occasionally using finger at points of difficulty							
Notices and uses punctuation to assist smooth reading							
Recognizes most words quickly and automatically							
Uses sound/letter relationships, known words, and word parts to figure out new words							
Uses meaning, visual information, and language syntax to figure out words							
Rereads to figure out words, self-correct, or improve phrasing and expression							
Rereads to search for meaning							
Remembers details to support the accumulation of meaning throughout the text							
Uses pictures for information but does not rely on them to make predictions							

GUIDED READING Text Types

USING THE
GUIDED READING PROGRAM

Characteristics of Text

Level H books are similar in difficulty to Level G, but Level H has a wider variety, including books with poetic or literary language. Sentences vary in length and difficulty, and some complex sentences carry over several pages. Children will need to be familiar with the syntactic patterns that occur.

Books have fewer repeating events and language patterns, requiring more control of aspects of print. The vocabulary is expanded and includes words that are less frequently used in oral language. The size of print varies widely.

Behaviors to Notice and Support

	Child's Name							
Reads fluently and rapidly, with appropriate phrasing								
Follows the text with eyes, using finger only at points of particular difficulty								
Notices and uses punctuation to assist smooth reading								
Recognizes most words rapidly								
Uses sound/letter relationships, known words, and word parts to figure out new words								
Uses meaning, visual information, and language syntax to solve problems								
Rereads phrases to figure out words, self-correct, or improve phrasing and expression								
Rereads to search for meaning								
Remembers details to support meaning accumulated through the text								
Uses pictures for information but does not rely on them to make predictions								
Searches for meaning while reading, stopping to think or talk about ideas								

LEVEL I

USING THE
GUIDED READING PROGRAM

Characteristics of Text

In general, the books at Level I are longer and more complex than at Levels G and H. The size of print is smaller and there are many more lines of print on the page. Books have longer sentences and paragraphs. There are more multisyllabic words, requiring complex word-solving skills. This level offers a greater variety of texts, including some that are informational, with technical language. Events in the text are more highly elaborated. Illustrations enhance the story, but provide low support for understanding meaning.

Behaviors to Notice and Support

	Child's Name							
Actively figures out new words, using a range of strategies								
Follows the print with eyes								
Reads fluently, slowing down to figure out new words and then resuming speed								
Begins to silently read some of the text								
In oral reading, rereads some words or phrases to self-correct or improve expression								
Rereads to search for meaning								
Flexibly uses meaning, language syntax, and visual information to figure out new words and to monitor reading								
Self-corrects errors that cause loss of meaning								
Rereads when necessary to self-correct, but not as a habit								
Demonstrates understanding of the story and characters								
Goes beyond the text in discussions and interpretations								
Sustains problem solving and development of meaning through a longer text and over a two- or three-day period								

USING THE
GUIDED READING PROGRAM

Characteristics of Text

Although it supports essentially the same reading behaviors, Level J offers books that are more difficult and varied than those at Level I. It includes informational books with new concepts and beginning chapter books with complex narratives and memorable characters. The amount of print varies; some Level J books have full pages of text with few illustrations. Generally, illustrations enhance the text but offer little support for understanding text meaning or figuring out new words. The difficulty of the language also varies. There are books with easy and familiar language and others with literary language or other challenges. Texts have many high-frequency words but may also have unfamiliar and/or technical words.

Behaviors to Notice and Support

	Child's Name							
Uses multiple sources of information to process text smoothly								
Uses multiple strategies to figure out new words while focusing on meaning								
Analyzes words from left to right, using knowledge of sound/letter relationships								
Uses known words and word parts to figure out new words								
Reads fluently, slowing down to figure out new words and then resuming speed								
Flexibly uses meaning, language syntax, and visual information to monitor reading								
Self-corrects errors that cause loss of meaning								
Rereads when necessary to self-correct, but not as a habit								
Rereads to search for meaning								
Demonstrates understanding of the story and characters								
Goes beyond the text in discussions and interpretations								
Sustains problem-solving and development of meaning through a longer text read over several days								
Silently reads sections of text								
Makes inferences, predicts, and analyzes character and plot								

LEVEL K

USING THE
GUIDED READING PROGRAM

Characteristics of Text

The Level K collection includes longer chapter books with memorable characters, shorter informational books with technical language and new concepts, and literary texts with illustrations that enhance meaning. Stories have multiple episodes related to a single plot. Some stories have to do with times, places, and characters outside children's experience.

Readers will need to use a variety of strategies to figure out new writing styles. At this level, most reading will be silent, although teachers will always sample oral reading or invite children to read aloud for emphasis or enjoyment in group sessions. It will take more than one sitting for children to read some of the longer chapter books.

Behaviors to Notice and Support

	Child's Name							
Integrates multiple sources of information while reading with fluency								
When reading orally, reads rapidly, with phrasing, slowing down to problem solve and then resuming speed								
Reads silently much of the time								
Demonstrates understanding of the text after silent reading								
Makes inferences, predicts, and analyzes character and plot								
Flexibly uses multiple word-solving strategies while focusing on meaning								
Goes beyond the text in understanding of problems and characters								
Demonstrates facility in interpreting the text								
Sustains attention to meaning and interpretation of a longer text read over several days								

USING THE GUIDED READING PROGRAM

Characteristics of Text

In general, reading behaviors for Level L are the same as for Level K except they are applied to longer and/or more complex books. At Level L there is greater variety of texts, including informational books, biographies, chapter books, and some longer, highly literary, or informational picture books.

Chapter books have more sophisticated plots and characters that are developed throughout the text. Some books have abstract or symbolic themes that require higher-level conceptual understandings. Texts contain an expanded vocabulary with many multisyllabic words.

Behaviors to Notice and Support

	Child's Name							
Integrates multiple sources of information while reading with fluency								
When reading orally, reads rapidly, with phrasing								
Reads orally, with accuracy, not stopping to self-correct in the interest of fluency and phrasing								
In oral reading, uses multiple word-solving strategies with longer words								
Reads silently most of the time								
Demonstrates understanding and facility in interpreting the text after silent reading								
After reading longer sections of a text, predicts events, outcomes, problem resolutions, and character changes								
Makes connections between the text read and other books								
Sustains attention to meaning and interpretation of a longer text read over several days								

USING THE
GUIDED READING PROGRAM

Characteristics of Text

Level M books have a variety of formats. Topics vary widely, and include subjects that will be familiar to students as well as those that are new. Literary selections have complex language and subtle meanings that require interpretation and background knowledge.

Chapter books are longer with few pictures. This requires readers to have mastery of the text. Many books have small print and little space between words. Vocabulary is expanded, and many words require background knowledge for comprehension.

Behaviors to Notice and Support

	Child's Name							
Uses multiple sources of information to figure out words rapidly while focusing on meaning								
Flexibly applies word-solving strategies to more-complex, multisyllabic words								
Demonstrates facility in interpreting text while reading orally, with fluency and phrasing								
Reads orally with high accuracy in most instances, not stopping to self-correct errors in the interest of fluency and phrasing								
Reads silently, except during assessment or to demonstrate text interpretation								
After reading longer sections of text, predicts outcomes, problem resolutions, and character changes								
Remembers details and sustains attention to meaning through a longer text								
Demonstrates understanding and facility at interpretation after silent reading								
Makes connections between the text read and other books								
Goes beyond the text to make more sophisticated interpretations								

USING THE
GUIDED READING PROGRAM

LEVEL N

Characteristics of Text

The Level N collection includes longer texts in a variety of genres. There are chapter books that present memorable characters developed through literary devices such as humor, irony, and whimsy. There are informational books and books that offer mystery and suspense. Level N also has shorter selections that provide opportunity to interpret texts and go beyond them. Vocabulary continues to expand, and topics go well beyond students' own experience.

Behaviors to Notice and Support

	Child's Name							
Uses multiple strategies to figure out new words quickly								
Demonstrates facility in text interpretation while reading orally, with fluency and phrasing								
Reads silently, except during assessment or when demonstrating text interpretation								
Remembers details from one section of text to the next								
Sustains attention to a longer text, remembering details and revising interpretations								
Notices how illustrations convey the author's meaning								
Demonstrates sophisticated interpretation of characters and plot								
Makes connections among a wide variety of texts								
Goes beyond the text to speculate on alternative meanings								

USING THE
GUIDED READING PROGRAM

Characteristics of Text

Books at Level O include selections from children's literature and chapter books. Books at this level explore more mature themes and topics that go beyond students' experience and expand it. Students can empathize with characters and learn about the lives of others. The vocabulary is sophisticated and varied. Most words will be known or within students' control; however, many will require interpretation of meaning. Many new multisyllabic words are included. Sentences are more complex and use a full range of punctuation.

Behaviors to Notice and Support

	Student's Name							
Solves words quickly and automatically while focusing on meaning								
Searches to understand the subtle shades of meaning that words can convey								
Demonstrates facility in text interpretation while reading orally, with fluency and phrasing								
In oral reading, figures out new words rapidly while reading smoothly and expressively								
Sustains attention to a text read over several days, remembering details and revising interpretations as new events are encountered								
After reading silently, demonstrates understanding and sophistication in text interpretation								
Makes connections among texts to enhance interpretation								
Goes beyond the text to speculate on alternative meanings								
Shows the ability to summarize the text in writing								

USING THE
GUIDED READING PROGRAM

Characteristics of Text

In general, books at this level are longer and ideas and language are more complex than at previous levels. Level P has a variety of informational texts, including history and biography. Through this variety, students become familiar with texts that are organized differently and learn how to gain information from them. Other genres include chapter books that explore the problems of early adolescence.

Behaviors to Notice and Support

	Student's Name							
When reading silently, reads rapidly and with attention to meaning								
Actively acquires new vocabulary through reading								
Demonstrates facility in text interpretation while reading orally, with fluency and phrasing								
In oral reading, figures out new words rapidly while reading smoothly and expressively								
Sustains attention to a text read over many days, remembering details and revising interpretations as new events are encountered								
Demonstrates interest in reading an extended text over a longer time period								
After reading silently, demonstrates understanding and sophistication in interpreting meaning								
Compares the text with other books in an analytic way								
Goes beyond the text to speculate on alternative meanings								
Shows the ability to summarize and extend the text in writing								

LEVEL Q

USING THE GUIDED READING PROGRAM

Characteristics of Text

Level Q includes literature selections with sophisticated humor, complex plots, and memorable characters. Themes at this level are sophisticated and require interpretation. They serve as a good foundation for group discussion. Illustrations and their relationship to the text can be examined as well. Books have complex structure and difficult words that offer challenges. There are some words from languages other than English. Longer texts require an extended time period to read.

Behaviors to Notice and Support

	Student's Name							
Reads rapidly, with attention to meaning, when reading silently								
Actively acquires new vocabulary through reading								
Demonstrates facility in text interpretation while reading orally, with fluency and phrasing								
In oral reading, figures out new words rapidly while reading smoothly and expressively								
Sustains attention to a text read over many days, remembering details and revising interpretations as new events are encountered								
Demonstrates interest in reading an extended text over a longer time period								
Uses illustrations to help analyze text meaning								
After reading silently, demonstrates understanding and sophistication in interpreting meaning								
Compares the text to other books in an analytic way								
Goes beyond the text to speculate on alternative meanings								
Goes beyond the text to interpret characters' thoughts and feelings								
Shows the ability to analyze and extend the text in writing								

USING THE
GUIDED READING PROGRAM

Characteristics of Text

At Level R, both fiction and nonfiction have a range of historical place and time settings, giving students an opportunity to empathize with characters and learn about their lives and the times and places in which they lived. In general, skills are the same as at Level Q, but are extended over a wider variety of texts. Some books require sustained reading over a longer time period. Vocabulary and language are sophisticated and offer challenges to the reader.

Behaviors to Notice and Support

Behaviors to Notice and Support	Student's Name							
Reads rapidly, both orally and silently, while focusing on meaning								
Actively acquires new vocabulary through reading								
Sustains attention to a text read over many days, remembering details and revising interpretations as new events are encountered								
Demonstrates interest in reading an extended text over a longer time period								
Extends the text in various ways, including through research								
Demonstrates interest and ability in interpreting shorter selections								
Uses illustrations to help analyze text meaning								
After reading silently, demonstrates understanding and sophistication in interpreting meaning								
Uses comparison with other texts to assist interpretation								
Goes beyond the text to interpret characters' thoughts and feelings and to speculate on alternative meanings								
Demonstrates all interpretive and analytic skills in writing								

LEVEL S

USING THE
GUIDED READING PROGRAM

Characteristics of Text

Level S includes literary selections, highly literary or informational picture books, and chapter books in a variety of genres. The collection reflects a wide variety of topics, cultures, and historical settings. Sentences and paragraphs at this level are complex.

Words present many shades of meaning which readers must interpret from the text and their own background knowledge. Selections offer opportunities for readers to make connections with other books they have read at earlier levels.

Behaviors to Notice and Support

	Student's Name							
Reads rapidly, both orally and silently, with attention to meaning								
Rapidly acquires new vocabulary through reading								
Sustains attention to a text read over many days, remembering details and revising interpretations as new events are encountered								
Demonstrates interest and ability in interpreting shorter selections								
Demonstrates flexibility in reading many different kinds of texts								
After reading silently, demonstrates understanding and sophistication in interpreting meaning								
Goes beyond the text to interpret characters' thoughts and feelings and to speculate on alternative meanings								
Demonstrates all analytic and interpretive skills in writing								
Extends text meaning through research, writing, or the arts								

USING THE
GUIDED READING PROGRAM

Characteristics of Text

The Level T collection has a great variety of genres. Short selections include informational books, legends, historical fiction, and folktales. Chapter books include autobiographies, historical narratives, realistic fiction, science fiction, and other fantasy stories. Some chapter books are quite long and require reading over an extended time. Judgment is needed as to whether students can sustain interest for these longer selections. Selections contain many sophisticated, multisyllabic words, and readers will need to consider both their literal and connotative meanings.

Behaviors to Notice and Support

	Student's Name							
Reads rapidly, both orally and silently, with attention to meaning								
In oral and silent reading, figures out new words automatically and easily interprets word meaning								
Sustains attention to a text read over many days, remembering details and revising interpretations as new events are encountered								
Demonstrates interest and ability in interpreting shorter selections								
Demonstrates flexibility in reading texts of different styles and genres								
After reading silently, demonstrates understanding and ability to analyze characters and plot								
Reflects knowledge of literary genre in conversation and writing								
Extends and demonstrates understanding of the text through writing in a variety of genres								
Extends and demonstrates understanding of the text through public speaking, research, or the arts								

USING THE
GUIDED READING PROGRAM

Characteristics of Text

Text at Level U requires readers to employ a wide range of sophisticated reading strategies that approach adult levels. The difference, of course, is that elementary and middle school students are still gaining the world experience and content knowledge, or the accumulation of text experience, needed to deeply understand the more complex texts they will be reading at Levels U through Z. By this time, students have built an integrated processing system, but they need to apply their strategies to increasingly difficult levels of text. As they do so, reading with fluency and understanding, they will expand and build their reading strategies.

Fiction texts at Level U may have several different themes and multiple story lines. Texts are increasingly literary, with writers expressing layers of meaning through symbolism. Themes are more abstract; creative formats may be used, such as collections of short stories that build meaning over different texts, or novels that incorporate diaries, poetry, or stories within stories. Generally, there are more characters to follow and their development is more complex; there are plots and subplots. Informational texts at Level U cover a wide range of topics and present specific, technical information. As with earlier levels, illustrations require interpretation and connection to text.

Behaviors to Notice and Support

	Student's Name							
Notices graphic illustrations and gets information from them								
Synthesizes information from graphic information with the body of the text								
Uses the table of contents to help in understanding the organization of the text								
Grasps "layers" of meaning in a story; for example, specific understandings plus the "bigger picture"								
Reads, understands, and appreciates literary language								
Interprets illustrations and their connections to the text								
Keeps up with several different themes and many characters								
Interprets characters' motives and the influences on their development								
Recognizes and appreciates a wide range of genres, both fiction and nonfiction								
Notices and uses a full range of punctuation, including more rarely used forms such as dashes								
Learns technical words from reading								
Uses reading to learn about self and others								

USING THE
GUIDED READING PROGRAM

Characteristics of Text

At Level V, readers employ essentially the same range of strategies as at the previous level, but more background knowledge will be required for true understanding. Also, students will be rapidly adding to their reading vocabularies. Fiction includes science fiction that presents sophisticated ideas and concepts. In many works of realistic or historical fiction, the writer is conveying a significant message beyond the story. Readers must think critically and sustain attention, memory, and understanding of theme over much longer texts. Full appreciation of texts requires noticing aspects of the writer's craft, including metaphor, simile, and symbolism. Many long texts have print in a much smaller font. Informational texts present complex ideas and may use language that is more technical. Topics are more often distant from students' experience in time and place. Biographies provide a significant amount of historical information. Many focus on harsh themes. Other, longer biographies are told in narrative style but present complex themes.

Behaviors to Notice and Support

	Student's Name						
Understands and talks about complex themes, analyzing them and applying them to current life situations							
Understands many different perspectives that are encountered in fiction and nonfiction texts							
Evaluates both fiction and nonfiction texts for their authenticity and accuracy							
Deals with mature topics such as death, war, prejudice, and courage							
Thinks critically about and discusses the content of a literary work or the quality of writing							
Notices aspects of the writer's craft and looks at the text from a writer's point of view							
Sustains attention and thinking over the reading of texts that are long and have smaller fonts							
Tries new genres, topics, and authors, and is able to compare them with known genres, topics, and authors							
Makes connections across texts to notice an author's style or technique							
Understands symbolism in both realistic fiction and fantasy; discusses what symbols mean in terms of today's society							
Brings prior knowledge to bear in understanding literary references							
Learns technical language and concepts through reading							
Learns about self and others through reading, especially about societies that are different from one's own							

USING THE
GUIDED READING PROGRAM

Characteristics of Text

Texts at Level W have themes that explore the human condition, with the same kinds of social problems mentioned at earlier levels. Fiction and nonfiction texts present characters who suffer hardship and learn from it. The writing is sophisticated, with complex sentences, literary language, and symbolism. Texts vary in length; print is generally in a small font. Comprehending texts at this level will require awareness of social and political issues; through them, readers can learn to understand current social problems at deeper levels.

Fantasy includes science fiction as well as "high" fantasy that introduces heroic characters, questions, and contests between good and evil. Informational texts may present complex graphic information and require readers to possess a wide range of content knowledge and to understand all of the basic organizational structures for nonfiction. Narrative-style biographies include many details of their subjects' lives and prompt readers to make inferences about what motivated their achievements.

Behaviors to Notice and Support

	Student's Name							
Sustains reading over longer and more complex texts; is not intimidated by varying layouts and styles of print								
Builds understanding of a wide variety of human problems								
Uses reading to expand awareness of people who are different from oneself								
Understands and learns from characters' experiences								
Learns about self and others through reading; actively seeks understanding of people different from oneself by culture, period of history, or other variation								
Deals with mature themes such as prejudice, war, death, survival, and poverty, and is able to discuss them in relation to one's own experiences								
Understands the complexities of human characters as they develop and change; discusses one's own point of view and relationship to characters								
Integrates understandings derived from graphic illustrations and the text								
Expands world knowledge through reading								
Flexibly and automatically uses tools such as glossary, references, index, credentials for authors, legends, charts, and diagrams								

USING THE
GUIDED READING PROGRAM

Characteristics of Text

Texts at Level X include the same wide range of genres shown at previous levels, but the themes explored are increasingly mature. Fantasy depicts quests and the struggle between good and evil. High fantasy includes complex, extended symbolic narratives that require knowledge of previously read texts for full understanding. Readers are required to go substantially beyond the literal meaning of the text to construct a writer's implied meaning. In addition, texts require interpretation of theme and plot. In fiction texts, there may be many characters to follow and understand. There is a continuing increase in the sophistication of vocabulary, language, and topics. Nonfiction texts require extensive prior knowledge for full understanding. In addition, texts are designed to present a great deal of new knowledge, sometimes in a dense way. Graphic illustrations are helpful to readers but also require interpretation.

Behaviors to Notice and Support

	Student's Name							
Sustains attention over longer texts with more abstract, mature, and complex themes								
Notices, understands, and discusses a wide range of literary devices, such as flashbacks and stories within stories								
Deals with mature themes, such as family relationships, death, social injustice, and the supernatural								
Appreciates, understands, and discusses irony and satire								
Uses descriptive text as a way to understand settings and their importance to the plot or character development								
Discusses the setting as an element of the text, deciding whether it is important or unimportant								
Flexibly and automatically uses tools such as glossary, references, index, credentials for authors, legends, charts, and diagrams								
Notices aspects of the author's craft, including the way characters are described and presented as "real"								
Talks about the text in an analytic way, including finding specific evidence of the author's style								
Understands and is able to use the sophisticated, scholarly, and technical language that is found in informational texts								

USING THE
GUIDED READING PROGRAM

Characteristics of Text

Books categorized as Level Y present subtle themes and complex plots. As with earlier levels, they include a whole range of social problems as themes, but more explicit details (for example, about death or prejudice) may be provided. Readers will need to bring considerable world experience and reading experience to their understanding of these more mature texts. Writers use symbolism, irony, satire, and other literary devices that require readers to think beyond the literal meaning of the text.

Books at Level Y include many more complex works of fantasy that depict hero figures and heroic journeys. Readers are required to discern underlying lessons and also to analyze texts for traditional elements. Informational texts explore an ever-widening world of history and science; topics require extensive prior knowledge of complex concepts, as well as vocabulary. Readers are required to gather new information from reading and synthesize it with their current knowledge. A wide range of critical reading skills are also required, so that students continuously evaluate the quality and objectivity of the texts they read.

Behaviors to Notice and Support

	Student's Name						
Understands and discusses subtle and complex plots and themes							
Understands, discusses, and deals in a mature way with a wide range of social problems, including social injustice and tragedy							
Understands and discusses in a mature way texts that present explicit details of social problems							
Understands literary irony and satire as they are used to communicate big ideas							
Understands complex fantasy, entering into whole new worlds, and understands concepts in relation to the imagined setting							
Understands and discusses the fact that words can have multiple meanings in relation to the context in which they are used							
Flexibly and automatically uses tools such as glossary, references, index, credentials for authors, legends, charts, and diagrams							
Interprets events in light of the setting—time, place, and culture							
Engages in critical thinking about fiction and nonfiction texts							
Critically evaluates nonfiction texts for accuracy and presentation of information							

Copyright © Scholastic Inc. All rights reserved.

120 Characteristics of Text

GUIDED READING Text Types

USING THE
GUIDED READING PROGRAM

Characteristics of Text

Level Z captures books that require reading strategies similar to those needed at lower levels, but which present such mature themes that readers simply need more experience to deal with them. Some students who are widely read may need this challenge. Some informational books present complex and technical information, sometimes within a denser text. Others deal with controversial social concepts and political issues that require readers to evaluate several points of view. Critical reading is essential, and readers often have to reevaluate and revise their own previously held beliefs. Historical texts have detailed accounts of periods of history that are less well known. Readers learn new ways of finding technical information, and encounter complex examples of the basic organizational structures for informational texts. Fiction texts explore a wide range of human themes, often with graphic details of hardship, violence, or tragedy. High fantasy presents heroic quests, symbolism, and complex characters, and involves the reader in considering the meaning of life.

Behaviors to Notice and Support

Student's Name								
Sustains reading and understanding over much longer texts								
Deals with a great range of texts—from diaries to narratives to plays								
Switches easily from one genre to another, accessing knowledge of the structure and nature of the text while beginning to read								
Understands and discusses how a text "works" in terms of the writer's organization								
Deals with controversial social and political issues, seeing multiple perspectives								
Uses reading to gain technical knowledge in a wide variety of areas								
Understands the symbolism in heroic quests; applies concepts encountered in fantasy to today's life								
Flexibly and automatically uses tools such as glossary, references, index, credentials for authors, legends, charts, and diagrams								
Deals with and discusses in a mature way graphic details such as accounts of brutality, hardship, or violence								
Notices, understands, appreciates, and discusses literary devices								
Understands and appreciates complex language, archaic language, and cultural motifs								
Learns about epilogues, bibliographies, and forewords								
Builds information across the text, even when very unusual formats are used (for example, brief interviews with many characters)								
Fully understands the subtle differences between fiction and nonfiction								

READING LOG

Child's Name

LEVEL A

Butterfly								
Fruit Salad								
Let's Go!								
My Mom								
The Rabbit House								
Sea Animals								
The Store								
The Three Frogs								
Time for Bed								
Up!								

LEVEL B

Building Blocks								
Buster and Ziggy								
Color It Blue								
Hats								
My Cat								
Party Time								
Polar Bears								
Puppy Paints								
School Fun								
Where Is Bob?								

LEVEL C

All Kinds of Pets								
Is It a Baby Animal?								
Let's Eat								
Mrs. Cat Goes Shopping								
My Costume								
Pig Played								
Ready Freddy								
The Sky								
Sleepy Bear								
Under the Umbrella								

GUIDED READING Text Types

READING LOG

Child's Name

LEVEL D

At the Toy Shop									
The Band									
A Day at the Beach									
Farm Helpers									
Ice Cream									
In the Desert									
Little Piglets									
Meet the Big Cats!									
Sand Animals									
Who Is Getting Married?									

LEVEL E

Bell									
Collections									
Eat Your Peas, Louise!									
Fish									
Fruit Trees									
I Love Rainy Days! (Noodles)									
Let's Play in the Forest While the Wolf Is Not Around!									
My New School									
Ring! Ring!									
Sammy the Turtle									

LEVEL F

Biscuit									
A Color of His Own									
A Day with Paramedics									
Does a Kangaroo Have a Mother, Too?									
Don't Be Late!									
Little Bird									
My River									
Popcorn									
Small Treasures									
Tina's Taxi									

READING LOG

	Child's Name								
LEVEL G									
Are We There Yet?									
A City Park									
Clifford Makes the Team									
Crafts									
Lost and Found									
Mousetrap									
The New Car									
Our Tree House									
Vegetable Soup									
Wake Up, Little Mouse!									
LEVEL H									
Canada									
Captain Cat									
I Need a Lunch Box									
Inside Mouse, Outside Mouse									
Just Me and My Dad (Little Critter)									
Larry and Loki									
Mom's Secret									
Now I Know: What's Under the Ocean?									
The Story of Henny Penny									
Too Late Harry!									
LEVEL I									
The Birthday Party									
Dragon Gets By									
Henry and Mudge and the Funny Lunch									
Hi! Fly Guy									
Now I Know: Bears									
Now I Know: Butterflies									
Small Pig									
The Very Busy Spider									
Who Wants a Ride?									
Willie's Wonderful Pet									

READING LOG

LEVEL J

	Child's Name								
Dig Dig Digging									
Have You Seen Duck?									
Henry and Mudge and the Best Day of All									
Hippo and Rabbit in Three Short Tales									
I Was So Mad (Little Critter)									
Log Hotel									
The Rain Came Down									
Story County									
The Wrong-way Rabbit									
Young Cam Jansen and the Baseball Mystery									

LEVEL K

10 Fat Turkeys									
Andy Shane and the Queen of Egypt									
Arthur's Eyes (An Arthur Adventure)									
Chicks and Salsa									
Dandelions: Stars in the Grass									
Earl the Squirrel									
Endangered Animals									
Frog and Toad All Year									
One Nosy Pup									
The Principal From the Black Lagoon									

LEVEL L

Amelia Bedelia, Rocket Scientist?									
Cam Jansen and the Chocolate Fudge Mystery									
Let's Read About ... George Washington									
Our Earth									
Ricky Ricotta's Mighty Robot vs. the Uranium Unicorns From Uranus									
Stand Tall, Molly Lou Melon									
The Subway Mouse									
Tony Baloney									
Whales Passing									
Worms for Lunch?									

READING LOG

	Child's Name								
LEVEL M									
Baby Animals									
The Case of the Groaning Ghost (A Jigsaw Jones Mystery)									
Class President (Marvin Redpost)									
Flat Stanley									
Goldilocks and the Three Bears									
The Lamb Who Came for Dinner									
Miss Smith's Incredible Storybook									
No Messin' with My Lesson (Katie Kazoo, Switcheroo)									
Oh No, It's Robert									
Who Eats What? Food Chains and Food Webs									
LEVEL N									
Blizzard of the Blue Moon (Magic Tree House)									
Brand-new School, Brave New Ruby (Ruby and the Booker Boys)									
Detective LaRue: Letters from the Investigation									
I Lost My Tooth in Africa									
Lunch Walks Among Us (Franny K. Stein, Mad Scientist)									
The Phantom Mudder (Jack Russell: Dog Detective)									
Sacajawea: Her True Story									
Why Mosquitoes Buzz in People's Ears									
You Can't Eat Your Chicken Pox, Amber Brown									
Young Frederick Douglass: Freedom Fighter									
LEVEL O									
Amelia Earhart: Adventure in the Sky									
Anansi Does the Impossible! An Ashanti Tale									
Clementine									
John Philip Duck									
Journey to the Volcano Palace (The Secrets of Droon)									
A Mouse Called Wolf									
Otis Spofford									
Teacher's Pet (Jake Drake)									
What's the Big Idea, Ben Franklin?									
You Can't Taste a Pickle With Your Ear									

READING LOG

Child's Name

LEVEL P

97 Ways to Train a Dragon (Dragon Slayers' Academy)								
Copper								
Gooseberry Park								
Happy Burger								
The Hunterman and the Crocodile								
Knights of the Kitchen Table (The Time Warp Trio)								
Kooks in the Cafeteria (Comic Guy)								
The Magic School Bus Explores the Senses								
My First Book of Biographies: Great Men and Women Every Child Should Know								
Tar Beach								

LEVEL Q

All About Manatees								
Book Two: The Stonekeeper's Curse (Amulet)								
The Clue at the Bottom of the Lake (Cabin Creek Mysteries)								
Finding the Titanic								
LaRue Across America: Postcards From the Vacation								
Magic Pickle and the Planet of the Grapes								
Nothing Ever Happens on 90th Street								
Shrek!								
Stallion in Spooky Hollow (Animal Ark)								
The Tale of Anton Brown and Grace Hopper								

LEVEL R

Clarice Bean Spells Trouble								
The Dragon of Lonely Island								
Episode Two: Invasion of the Relatives (Julian Rodriguez)								
Freedom Crossing								
Magic Pickle: The Full Color Graphic Novel!								
Miracles on Maple Hill								
Owen & Mzee: The True Story of a Remarkable Friendship								
Sitting Down for Dr. King								
What to Do About Alice?								
Who Cracked the Liberty Bell?								

READING LOG

Child's Name

LEVEL S

Amelia Earhart: This Broad Ocean									
Confessions of a Gym-Class Dropout									
The Dinosaurs of Waterhouse Hawkins									
From the Mixed-Up Files of Mrs. Basil E. Frankweiler									
The Good Dog									
The Houdini Box									
Out of Darkness: The Story of Louis Braille									
Taking Sides									
When Women Played Baseball									
The Young Man and the Sea									

LEVEL T

Colonial Times: 1600–1700									
The Dodgeball Chronicles (Knights of the Lunch Table)									
It Only Looks Easy									
Life in the Oceans: Animals, People, Plants									
Mudshark									
Sir Arthur Conan Doyle's The Red-Headed League									
Smile									
Tracker									
The Word Eater									
The Wright 3									

LEVEL U

The BFG									
The Calder Game									
The Extraordinary Mark Twain (According To Susy)									
The Fairy-Tale Detectives (The Sisters Grimm)									
My Side of the Mountain									
Road to Revolution!									
The Ruins of Gorlan (Ranger's Apprentice)									
Sir Arthur Conan Doyle's Sherlock Holmes and the Blue Carbuncle									
The Star Crusher (Missile Mouse)									
Wringer									

GUIDED READING Text Types

READING LOG

Child's Name

LEVEL V

The Bad Beginning (A Series of Unfortunate Events)										
Black Star, Bright Dawn										
The Capture (Guardians of Ga'hoole)										
The Cats in Krasinski Square										
Double-Dare to Be Scared: Another Thirteen Chilling Tales										
Ghostopolis										
Heat										
Lewis Carroll's Alice in Wonderland										
Sojourner Truth: Ain't I a Woman?										
The Titanic										

LEVEL W

The Great Cow Race (Bone)										
Houdini: The Handcuff King										
I Am a Star: Child of the Holocaust										
Max the Mighty: A Novel										
Mind Readers: Science Examines ESP										
Numbering All the Bones										
The Phantom Tollbooth										
Stowaway										
The Titan's Curse (Percy Jackson & the Olympians)										
Torn Thread										

LEVEL X

Any Small Goodness: A Novel of the Barrio										
Elijah of Buxton										
Harlem Summer										
King George III: America's Enemy										
The Legend of Hong Kil Dong: The Robin Hood of Korea										
The Little Prince										
The Mostly True Adventures of Homer P. Figg										
O. Henry's The Gift of the Magi										
Satchel Paige: Striking Out Jim Crow										
Stanford Wong Flunks Big-Time										

READING LOG

Child's Name

LEVEL Y

All the Broken Pieces									
Artemis Fowl: The Graphic Novel									
Bad Boy: A Memoir									
Children of the Dust Bowl									
The Devil's Arithmetic									
Jackaroo: A Novel in the Kingdom									
Milkweed									
Riot									
Truce									
Weedflower									

LEVEL Z

Chains									
Chasing Lincoln's Killer									
Countdown									
The Evolution of Calpurnia Tate									
The Glass Menagerie									
The Hunger Games									
The Many Rides of Paul Revere									
Stormbreaker: The Graphic Novel (Alex Rider)									
Tales From Outer Suburbia									
Uglies									

EVALUATION RESPONSE FOR TEXT GRADIENT

adapted from *Guided Reading: Good First Teaching for All Children* (Fountas and Pinnell, 1996)

Directions: Since any gradient is always in the process of construction when it is used with varying groups of students, we expect our list to change every year. We encourage you to try the levels with your students and to provide feedback based on your own experiences. Please suggest changes to existing book levels and suggest new books for the list. Please provide the information requested.

Name: _____ **Grade Level You Teach:** _____

Telephone: _____ **E-mail Address:** _____

Address: _____

Book Evaluated

Book Title: _____ **Level:** _____

Author: _____ **Publisher:** _____

This book is

_____ A book that I have evaluated by using it with my class.

To what level should it be moved? _____

Why? _____

_____

_____ A book that I am recommending as a benchmark book.

How does it support readers at this level? _____

What challenge does it offer? _____

_____

_____ A new book that I am recommending to the collection.

At what level should it be placed? _____

Why? _____

_____

Copy and mail this form to:
Irene C. Fountas
Lesley University
Suite 2-029
1815 Massachusetts Avenue
Cambridge, MA 02140

ADDITIONAL LEVELED BOOKS AVAILABLE FROM SCHOLASTIC

Level A

Big and Little
by Samantha Berger

I Am
by Adria Klein

Kittens
by Don L. Curry

What Bears Like
by Janelle Cherrington

My Color
by Rachel Mann

What Do Insects Do?
by Susan Canizares

Level B

Dogs
by Amy Levin

Goldilocks
by Dom Deluise

Kites
by Bettina Ling

Lunch at the Zoo
by Wendy Blaxland

Monkeys
by Susan Canizares and
Pamela Chanko

We Like to Play!
by Ellen Tarlow

Level C

Bo and Peter
by Betsy Franco

I Can Run
by Gay Su Pinnell

In the City
by Susana Pasternac

How Many Can Play?
by Susan Canizares and
Betsey Chessen

Little Sister
by Robin Mitchell

*Pancakes, Crackers, and Pizza:
A Book of Shapes*
by Margaret Gisler and
Marjorie Eberts

Level D

Don't Be Late!
by Akimi Gibson

The Haircut
by Armstrong & Hartley

I Love Mud and Mud Loves Me
by Vicki Stephens

I Know Karate
by Mary Packard

One Happy Classroom
by Chaman Simon

Too Many Balloons
by Catherine Matthias

Where Do Birds Live?
by Betsey Chessen

Level E

A Box Can Be Many Things
by Dana Meachen Rau

A Buzz Is Part of a Bee
by Carolyn Lunn

Look, I Can Read!
by Susan Hood

Just a Seed
by Wendy Blaxland

Tortillas
by Margarita González-Jensen

A Tree Can Be . . .
by Judy Nayer

The Voyage of Mae Jemison
by Susan Canizares and
Samantha Berger

Level F

Amy Loves the Snow
by Julia Hoban

Cookie's Week
by Cindy Ward

I Am Fire
by Jean Marzollo

Itchy, Itchy Chicken Pox
by Grace Maccarone

My Dog's the Best
by Stephanie Calmenson

Shine, Sun!
by Carol Greene

"What Is That?" Said the Cat
by Grace Maccarone

Level G

All About You
by Catherine and
Laurence Anholt

Buzz Said the Bee
by Wendy Cheyette Lewison

How Have I Grown?
by Mary Reid

Make It Move
by Susan Canizares and
Betsey Chessen

Sam the Garbage Hound
by Charnan Simon

Sometimes Things Change
by Patricia Eastman

Level H

*A Clean House for Mole and
Mouse*
by Harriet Ziefert

I Was Walking Down the Road
by Sarah Barchas

Mr. McCready's Cleaning Day
by Tracey Shilling

My Pigs
by Heather Miller

Plane Rides
by Pamela Walker

What Will the Weather Be Like Today?
by Paul Rogers

Level I

The Blue Mittens
by Rachel Mann

Did You See Chip?
by Wong Herbert Yee

Henny Penny
by H. Werner Zimmermann

Messy Bessy's Family Reunion
by Patricia C. McKissack

Red-Eyed Tree Frog
by Joy Cowley

We Just Moved!
by Stephen Krensky

Level J

Bear's Bargain
by Frank Asch

Big Mama and Grandma Ghana
by Angela Shelf Medearis

Clifford the Big Red Dog
by Norman Bridwell

Insects
by Carolyn MacLulich

Me on the Map
by Joan Sweeney

On the Lake
by Liane Onish

Poppleton Everyday
by Cynthia Rylant

Level K

Amalia and the Grasshopper
by Jerry Tello

Bedtime for Frances
by Russell Hoban

The Blind Men and the Elephant
by Karen Backstein

The Bremen-Town Musicians
by Ruth Belov Gross

Ming Lo Move Mountains
by Arnold Lobel

A Place for Grace
by Jean Davies Okimoto

What Magnets Can Do
by Allan Fowler

Level L

Apatosaurus
by Elaine Landau

Black Bear Cub
by Alan Lind

Happy Birthday, Martin Luther King
by Jean Marzollo

Horrible Harry and the Ant Invasion
by Suzy Kline

The Mud Pony
by Caron Lee Cohen

Play Ball, Amelia Bedelia
by Peggy Parish

Solve it!
by Meish Goldish

Level M

Boom!
by Howard Gunter

California or Bust!
by Judith Bauer Stamper

Cloudy With a Chance of Meatballs
by Judi Barrett

George Washington's Mother
by Jean Fritz

The Littles Go Exploring
by John Lawrence Peterson

Nine True Dolphin Stories
by Margaret Davidson

Level N

The Cat Who Wore a Pot on Her Head
by Jan Slepian & Ann Seidler

Catwings Return
by Ursula K. Le Guin

Do Tornadoes Really Twist?
by Melvin Berger

The Garden on Green Street
by Meish Goldish

How Is a Crayon Made?
by Oz Charles

Tikki Tikki Tembo
by Arlene Mosel

Level O

The Boxcar Children #1
by Gertrude Warner Chandler

The Cat's Meow
by Gary Soto

Class Clown
by Johanna Hurwitz

ADDITIONAL LEVELED BOOKS AVAILABLE FROM SCHOLASTIC

Desert Life
by Rachel Mann

Flossie and the Fox
by Patricia C. McKissack

Miss Rumphius
by Barbara Cooney

A Picture Book of Sojourner Truth
by Anne F. Rockwell

Level P

26 Fairmont Avenue
by Tomie dePaola

The Adventures of Captain Underpants
by Dav Pilkey

The Eagle Has Landed
by Peter Merchant

Shoebag
by Mary James

A Whale Is Not a Fish
by Melvin Berger

Wanted Dead or Alive: The True Story of Harriet Tubman
by Ann McGovern

Level Q

American Tall Tales
by Mary Pope Osborne

Animals of Long Ago
by Susan Ring

Exploring the Titanic
by Robert D. Ballard

Great Black Heroes: Five Brave Explorers
by Wade Hudson

Mary On Horseback
by Rosemary Wells

The True Story of the 3 Little Pigs
by Jon Scieszka

Level R

Brian's Winter
by Gary Paulsen

A Jar of Dreams
by Yoshiko Uchida

The Last Princess
by Fay Stanley

Listening to Crickets
by Candice F. Ransom

Run Away Home
by Patricia C. McKissack

They Came From Center Field
by Dan Gutman

Level S

Afternoon of the Elves
by Janet Taylor Lisle

Ben and Me
by Robert Lawson

The Broccoli Tapes
by Jan Slepian

The Chicago Fire
by Howard Gutner

Eureka! It's Television!
by Jeanne Bendick

The Young Man and the Sea
by Rodman Philbrick

Level T

Bridge to Terabithia
by Katherine Paterson

The Big Lie: A True Story
by Isabella Leitner

The Girl Who Chased Sorrow
by Ann Turner

Sounder
by Jeanette Sanderson and William Howard Armstrong

The Story of Levi's
by Michael Burgan

Level U

Bad, Badder, Baddest
by Cynthia Voigt

Ella Enchanted
by Gail Carson Levine

Geysers: When the Earth Roars
by Roy A. Gallant

Hoang Anh
by Diane Goldsmith

An Indian Winter
by Russell Freedman

The Secret Garden
by Frances Hodgson Burnett

Level V

1000 Facts About Space
by Pam Beasant

Alice In Wonderland
by Lewis Carroll

The Golden Goblet
by Eloise Jarvis McGraw

Harry Potter and the Chamber of Secrets
by J. K. Rowling

The Music of the Dolphins
by Karen Hesse

The Secret of NIMH
by Robert C. O'Brien

Level W

Buried In Ice
by Owen Beattie

The Great Fire
by Jim Murphy

The First Woman Doctor
by Rachel Baker

*John and Abigail Adams:
An American Love Story*
by Judith St. George

Maniac Magee
by Jerry Spinelli

The Moon Bridge
by Marcia Savin

The Phantom Tollbooth
by Norton Juster

Level X

*13 Ghosts: Strange but True
Stories*
by Will Osborne

Anne Frank: Beyond the Diary
by Rian Verhoeven

Call It Courage
by Armstrong Sperry

Children of the Wild West
by Russell Freedman

The Iceberg Hermit
by Arthur Roth

One More River to Cross
by Jim Haskins

Pyramid
by David Macaulay

*Zlata's Diary: A Child's Life in
Sarajevo*
by Zlata Filipovic

Level Y

Blizzard!
by Jim Murphy

The Call of the Wild
by Jack London, with an
introduction by Avi

Confucius: The Golden Rule
by Russell Freedman

*The Day Martin Luther King, Jr.
Was Shot*
by James Haskins

*I Am An American: A True Story
of Japanese Internment*
by Jerry Stanley

The Ear, the Eye, and the Arm
by Nancy Farmer

*Now Is Your Time! The African-
American Struggle for Freedom*
by Walter Dean Myers

Level Z

Black Beauty
by Anna Sewell

The Day Women Got the Vote
by George Sullivan

*The Journal of Patrick Seamus
Flaherty: United States Marine
Corps, Khe Sanh, Vietnam, 1968*
by Ellen Emerson White

The Raven and Other Poems
by Edgar Allan Poe

*Red Scarf Girl: A Memoir of a
Cultural Revolution*
by Ji-li Jiang

Tom Sawyer
by Mark Twain

Treasure Island
by Robert Louis Stevenson

Dear Family Member:

Your child is becoming a skilled independent reader! And the guided reading books that your reader will bring home are designed to help in this process.

As part of the *Scholastic Guided Reading Program,* your child will participate in small groups and will receive individualized instruction to develop fluency, oral language, vocabulary, phonics, comprehension, and writing skills. In addition, your child will bring home enjoyable, level-appropriate stories and selections that will help to ensure his or her success as an independent reader.

Here are some suggestions for helping your child before, during, and after reading:

Before

- Look at the book cover with your child. Together, review the illustrations or photographs in the book. Ask your child to predict what the story or selection will be about.

- Discuss what you and your child might already know about the topic of the book you are about to read.

- If your child is a beginning reader, echo-read the story or selection with your child by reading a line first and having your child read it after you. If your child is a more skilled reader, periodically stop and ask questions.

During

- If your child does not recognize a word right away, help him or her to focus on the familiar letters and spelling patterns in the word. Guide your child to think about other words that look like the unfamiliar word.

- Encourage your child to use phonics and decoding skills to sound out any new, unfamiliar words. If necessary, provide the word if your child struggles.

- Encourage your child to read with expression and to enjoy reading!

After

- Encourage your child to reread the story or selection to develop confidence. If the book is long, reread a few favorite sections or chapters. Perhaps your child could read the story or selection to other family members or friends.

- Discuss the story or selection with your child. Ask questions such as: What were your favorite parts? Who were your favorite characters? Why? What interesting fact did you learn?

- Have your child keep a journal of favorite stories and selections and interesting words in those books. Your child might also like to write about the book in this journal.

Have fun with this reading experience and your child will have fun, too!

Sincerely,

Estimado padre o tutor:

Su niño está en el proceso de convertirse en un lector hábil e independiente. Los libros de lectura guiada que su niño llevará a casa han sido concebidos para ayudar en este proceso.

Como parte del Programa de Lectura Guiada de Scholastic, su niño participará en grupos pequeños y recibirá instrucción individualizada con el objetivo de desarrollar la fluidez, el lenguaje oral, el vocabulario, la fonética, la comprensión y las destrezas de escritura. Además, su niño llevará a casa lecturas amenas y apropiadas a su nivel, que le servirán para garantizar su éxito como lector independiente.

Éstas son algunas sugerencias para ayudar a su niño antes, durante y después de la lectura:

Antes

- Observe con su niño la cubierta del libro. Repasen juntos las ilustraciones o fotografías del libro. Pídale a su niño predecir de qué tratará el cuento o la selección que van a leer.

- Comenten lo que usted y su niño ya sepan sobre el tema del libro que van a leer.

- Si su niño es un lector principiante, lea usted primero una línea y pídale que lea esa misma línea después. Si su niño es un lector más avanzado, haga una pausa de vez en cuando para hacerle preguntas.

Durante

- Si a su niño le resulta difícil reconocer alguna palabra, ayúdelo a fijarse en las letras y patrones ortográficos con los que esté familiarizado. Guíe a su niño en la búsqueda de otras palabras que se parezcan a la palabra desconocida.

- Anime a su niño a usar la fonética y las destrezas de decodificación para leer en voz alta cualquier palabra nueva o desconocida. Si su niño tiene dificultades para hacerlo de manera independiente, lea usted la palabra.

- Anime a su niño a leer de manera expresiva y a disfrutar de la lectura.

Después

- Anime a su niño a volver a leer el cuento o la selección para que gane confianza como lector. Si el libro es demasiado largo, vuelva a leer algunas de las secciones o pasajes favoritos. También puede pedirle que lea el cuento a otros familiares o amigos.

- Comente con su niño el cuento o la selección. Hágale preguntas como las siguientes: ¿Qué partes te gustaron más? ¿Qué personajes son tus favoritos? ¿Por qué? ¿Qué hecho o dato importante aprendiste leyendo este libro?

- Pídale que lleve un récord de sus cuentos y selecciones favoritos, así como de las palabras interesantes que encuentre en los mismos. También, puede llevar un diario con comentarios sobre los libros.

Disfrute de la lectura. ¡Su niño, de seguro, también disfrutará!

Atentamente,

GRADE K: REPRODUCIBLE FICTION BOOKMARKS

Share these bookmarks with your children to remind them of some key features of different fiction genres/ text types.

Reading Realistic Fiction

- ✓ Look at the cover.
- ✓ Say the name of the book.
- ✓ Look at the pictures.
- ✓ See who is in the story.
- ✓ See what they do.
- ✓ Read the story.
- ✓ Think about what happens first, next, last.

Reading a Fairy Tale

- ✓ Say the name of the book.
- ✓ Flip through the book.
- ✓ Look for things that are not real.
- ✓ Read the story.
- ✓ Think about where the story takes place.
- ✓ Look for a happy ending.

Reading a Poem

- ✓ Read the name of the poem.
- ✓ Read the poem aloud.
- ✓ Hear words that sound the same.
- ✓ Hear a pattern.
- ✓ Think about the words.

Reading a Fantasy

- ✓ Look at the cover.
- ✓ Say the name of the book.
- ✓ Look at the pictures.
- ✓ Look for things that could not happen in real life.

MARCADORES REPRODUCIBLES/GÉNERO FICCIÓN

Reparta estos marcadores entre sus alumnos para que recuerden algunas de las características del texto en el género ficción.

Al leer un cuento de ficción realista

✓ Mira la portada.

✓ Di el nombre del libro.

✓ Mira los dibujos.

✓ Mira quiénes participan en el cuento. Mira qué hacen.

✓ Lee el cuento.

✓ Piensa en qué pasa primero, al medio y al final.

Al leer un cuento de hadas

✓ Di el nombre del libro.

✓ Hojea el libro.

✓ Busca cosas que no sean reales.

✓ Lee el cuento.

✓ Piensa en dónde ocurre el cuento.

✓ Busca el final feliz.

Al leer un poema

✓ Lee el nombre del poema.

✓ Lee el poema en voz alta.

✓ Pon atención a las palabras que suenen parecidas.

✓ Pon atención al patrón de la rima.

✓ Piensa en las palabras.

Al leer un cuento de fantasía

✓ Mira la portada.

✓ Di el nombre del libro.

✓ Mira los dibujos.

✓ Busca cosas que no podrían ocurrir en la vida real.

GRADE 1: REPRODUCIBLE FICTION BOOKMARKS

Share these bookmarks with your children to remind them of some key features of different fiction genres/text types.

Reading Realistic Fiction

✓ Look at the cover.

✓ Read the title.

✓ Look at the pictures.

✓ See who is in the story. See what they do.

✓ Read the story.

✓ Think about what happens first, next, last.

Reading a Fairy Tale

✓ Read the title.

✓ Flip through the book.

✓ Look for places, people, and animals that are not real.

✓ Read the story.

✓ Think about where the story takes place.

✓ Think about when the story takes place.

✓ Look for a happy ending.

Reading a Poem

✓ Read the title. Find out what the poem is about.

✓ Read the poem aloud.

✓ Listen for words that rhyme.

✓ Listen for a pattern in the words.

✓ Think about the pictures that the words make in your mind.

Reading Fantasy

✓ Read the title.

✓ Flip through the book.

✓ Look for things that could not happen in real life.

✓ Look for places that could not be real.

✓ Look for animals that act like people and talk in the story.

MARCADORES REPRODUCIBLES/GÉNERO FICCIÓN

Reparta estos marcadores entre sus alumnos para que recuerden algunas de las características del texto en el género ficción.

Al leer un cuento de ficción realista

✓ Mira la portada.

✓ Lee el título.

✓ Mira los dibujos.

✓ Mira quiénes participan en el cuento. Mira qué hacen.

✓ Lee el cuento.

✓ Piensa en qué pasa primero, al medio y al final.

Al leer un cuento de hadas

✓ Lee el título.

✓ Hojea el libro.

✓ Busca lugares, personas y animales que no sean reales.

✓ Lee el cuento.

✓ Piensa en dónde ocurre el cuento.

✓ Piensa en cuándo ocurre el cuento.

✓ Busca el final feliz.

Al leer un poema

✓ Lee el título. Descubre de qué trata el poema.

✓ Lee el poema en voz alta.

✓ Pon atención a las palabras que riman.

✓ Busca un patrón en las palabras.

✓ Piensa en las cosas que te imaginas al leer.

Al leer un cuento de fantasía

✓ Lee el título.

✓ Hojea el libro.

✓ Busca cosas que no podrían ocurrir en la vida real.

✓ Busca lugares que no podrían ser reales.

✓ Busca animales que actúen como personas y que hablen.

GRADE 2: REPRODUCIBLE FICTION BOOKMARKS

Share these bookmarks with your children to remind them of some of the key features of different fiction genres/text types.

Quick Clues for Reading Realistic Fiction

✓ Look at the cover.
✓ Read the title.
✓ Look for people in the story who are like real people.
✓ Read where the story happens, such as a school or a home.
✓ Find out what people do to fix problems.

Quick Clues for Reading a Fairy Tale

✓ Read the title.
✓ Look at the pictures. Look for places, people, and animals that are not real.
✓ Read the story.
✓ Read to find out where the story takes place.
✓ Think about when the story happens.
✓ Look for a happy ending.

Quick Clues for Reading a Mystery

✓ Read the title to find out what the mystery is.
✓ Read the story. Find out the puzzle or crime. See who wants to solve it.
✓ Look for clues to solve the mystery.
✓ Think about what will happen next.

Quick Clues for Reading a Poem

✓ Read the title. Find out what the poem is about.
✓ Read the poem aloud.
✓ Listen for a pattern in the sentences.
✓ Listen for a pattern in the words.
✓ Think about the pictures the words make in your mind.

Quick Clues for Reading a Fable

✓ Read the title. Look for names of animals.
✓ Read the story. See how the animals or objects talk.
✓ Read the end. Find out what happens to one of the animals.
✓ Think about the lesson learned.

Quick Clues for Reading Fantasy

✓ Look for people, animals, and places that are not real.
✓ Find out if there are animals that talk or people who travel in time.
✓ Find out what the problem is.
✓ Read to see how the problem is solved.

MARCADORES REPRODUCIBLES/GÉNERO FICCIÓN

Reparta estos marcadores entre sus alumnos para que recuerden algunas de las características del texto en el género ficción.

Breves consejos para leer textos de ficción realista

✓ Mira la portada.

✓ Lee el título.

✓ En el cuento, busca personas que sean como las personas de verdad.

✓ Lee dónde ocurre la historia, por ejemplo, en una escuela o una casa.

✓ Descubre qué hace la gente para resolver los problemas.

Breves consejos para leer un cuento de hadas

✓ Lee el título.

✓ Mira los dibujos. Busca lugares, personas y animales que no sean reales.

✓ Lee el cuento.

✓ Lee para saber dónde ocurre la historia.

✓ Piensa en cuándo ocurre la historia.

✓ Busca el final feliz.

Breves consejos para leer un cuento de misterio

✓ Lee el título para saber de qué trata el misterio.

✓ Lee el cuento. Descubre el acertijo o el crimen. Descubre quién quiere resolverlo.

✓ Busca pistas para resolver el misterio.

✓ Piensa en qué ocurrirá después.

Breves consejos para leer un poema.

✓ Lee el título. Descubre de qué trata el poema.

✓ Lee el poema en voz alta.

✓ Busca un patrón en las oraciones.

✓ Busca un patrón en las palabras.

✓ Piensa en las cosas que te imaginas al leer.

Breves consejos para leer una fábula

✓ Lee el título. Busca nombres de animales.

✓ Lee la historia. Fíjate en cómo hablan los animales o los objetos.

✓ Lee el final. Descubre qué le ocurre a uno de los animales.

✓ Piensa en la lección aprendida.

Breves consejos para leer un cuento de fantasía

✓ Busca personas, animales y lugares que no sean reales.

✓ Fíjate en si hay animales que hablan o gente que viaja en el tiempo.

✓ Descubre cuál es el problema.

✓ Lee para saber cómo se resuelve el problema.

GRADE 3: REPRODUCIBLE FICTION BOOKMARKS

Share these bookmarks with your students to remind them of some key features of different fiction genres/text types.

Quick Clues for Reading Realistic Fiction

✓ Look at the cover and the title.

✓ Read the story. See if the characters are like real people.

✓ Look for where and when the story happens. See if it's like a real place.

✓ Read where the story happens, such as a school or a home.

✓ Find out what people do to solve their problems.

Quick Clues for Reading a Folktale

✓ Read the title. Think what the story is about.

✓ Read the story. See which characters are good and which are bad.

✓ Find out what the characters' goals are.

✓ Look for things that happen three times.

✓ Find out if the good characters reach their goals in the end. See what happens to the bad characters.

Quick Clues for Reading a Mystery

✓ Read the title to learn what the mystery is.

✓ Read the story to find the puzzle or crime and who wants to solve it.

✓ Look for clues to solve the mystery.

✓ Think about events that are scary and can't be explained.

✓ Look for clues that help you guess what will happen next.

✓ See how the mystery is solved in the end.

Quick Clues for Reading a Poem

✓ Read the title. Think about what the topic of the poem is.

✓ Look at how many lines there are and if they are in groups.

✓ Read the poem aloud.

✓ Listen for a pattern in the words.

✓ Listen for a pattern in the sentences.

✓ Think about the pictures that form in your mind as you read.

Quick Clues for Reading a Play

✓ Read the title.

✓ Find a list of characters in the beginning.

✓ Read each act or part of the play. Note where each act takes place.

✓ Look for the names of characters and the words they say.

✓ Look for words that tell you how the characters speak and move.

Quick Clues for Reading Fantasy

✓ Read the title. Think what it tells you about the story.

✓ Read the story. Look for people, places, and animals that are not real.

✓ Look for animals that may talk and people who may travel in time.

✓ Find out what the problem is.

✓ Read to see how the problem is solved and if magic or magical thinking is used.

MARCADORES REPRODUCIBLES/GÉNERO FICCIÓN

Reparta estos marcadores entre sus alumnos para que recuerden algunas de las características del texto en el género ficción.

Breves consejos para leer ficción realista

✓ Mira la portada y el título.

✓ Lee el cuento. Fíjate si los personajes son como las personas de verdad.

✓ Busca dónde y cuándo ocurre la historia. Piensa en si es como un lugar real.

✓ Lee dónde ocurre la historia, por ejemplo, en una escuela o una casa.

✓ Averigua qué hace la gente para resolver los problemas.

Breves consejos para leer un cuento folclórico

✓ Lee el título. Piensa sobre qué trata el cuento.

✓ Lee el cuento. Piensa en qué personajes son buenos y cuáles son malos.

✓ Descubre cuáles son las metas de los personajes.

✓ Busca cosas que ocurran tres veces.

✓ Descubre si al final los personajes buenos alcanzan sus metas. Lee qué les ocurre a los personajes malos.

Breves consejos para leer un cuento de misterio

✓ Lee el título para saber de qué trata el misterio.

✓ Lee el cuento para hallar el acertijo o problema y quiénes desean resolverlo.

✓ Busca pistas para resolver el misterio.

✓ Piensa en los eventos aterradores que no se puedan explicar.

✓ Busca pistas para adivinar qué va a ocurrir.

✓ Descubre cómo se resuelve el misterio al final del cuento.

Breves consejos para leer un poema

✓ Lee el título. Piensa en cuál es el tema del poema.

✓ Mira cuántas líneas tiene el poema y si están en grupos.

✓ Lee el poema en voz alta.

✓ Busca un patrón en las palabras.

✓ Busca un patrón en las oraciones.

✓ Piensa en qué te imaginas al leer el poema.

Breves consejos para leer una obra de teatro

✓ Lee el título.

✓ Busca la lista de personajes al principio de la obra.

✓ Lee todos los actos o partes de la obra. Fíjate en dónde ocurre cada acto.

✓ Busca los nombres de los personajes y lo que dicen.

✓ Busca palabras que te indiquen cómo hablan y se mueven los personajes.

Breves consejos para leer un cuento de fantasía

✓ Lee el título. Piensa en qué te indica sobre el cuento.

✓ Lee el cuento. Busca personas, lugares y animales que no sean reales.

✓ Busca animales que hablen o personas que viajen en el tiempo.

✓ Descubre cuál es el problema.

✓ Lee para saber cómo se resuelve el problema y si se usó magia para hacerlo.

GRADE 4: REPRODUCIBLE FICTION BOOKMARKS

Share these bookmarks with your students to remind them of some key features of different fiction genres/ text types.

Quick Clues for Reading Realistic Fiction

✓ Read the title. Think what the cover shows.

✓ Read the story. Meet the characters and learn about the setting.

✓ Note how characters are like real people with real problems.

✓ Follow the sequence of events. Predict what will happen next.

✓ Find out what people do to solve problems or reach goals.

Quick Clues for Reading a Novel

✓ Read the title and the author's name.

✓ Check how many chapters there are.

✓ Note the setting and the time covered by the story as you read.

✓ Note the main characters and what they are like.

✓ Follow the events, problems, and conflicts in the plot.

✓ Note how problems are solved in the end.

Quick Clues for Reading a Mystery

✓ Read the title to learn what the mystery is.

✓ Note the characters who want to solve the mystery and why.

✓ Look for clues to solve the mystery.

✓ Look for how the author builds suspense.

✓ Look for clues that help you guess what will happen next.

✓ See how the mystery is solved in the end.

Quick Clues for Reading Historical Fiction

✓ Read the title and the author's name.

✓ Note when and where in history the story takes place.

✓ Read the story. Imagine how people lived in this time.

✓ See how characters take part in historical events.

✓ Compare how people in the past solve problems with what people do today.

Quick Clues for Reading a Play

✓ Read the title and the playwright's name.

✓ Read the list of characters' names in the beginning.

✓ Note where each act of the play takes place.

✓ Look for characters' names before the words they say.

✓ Note words that explain how the characters speak and move.

Quick Clues for Reading a Graphic Novel

✓ Read the title and author's name.

✓ Preview the pictures, or graphic part of the novel, before you start reading.

✓ Find characters' words in the speech balloons.

✓ Look for how characters feel in the illustrations.

✓ Find descriptions of what happens in the text boxes on the illustrations.

✓ Follow the story sequence by moving from panel to panel.

MARCADORES REPRODUCIBLES/GÉNERO FICCIÓN

Reparta estos marcadores entre sus alumnos para que recuerden algunas de las características del texto en el género ficción.

Breves consejos para leer ficción realista

✓ Lee el título. Piensa en qué muestra la portada.

✓ Lee el cuento. Conoce los personajes y aprende sobre el escenario.

✓ Fíjate que los personajes son como las personas reales y que tienen problemas de verdad.

✓ Sigue la secuencia de sucesos. Predice qué ocurrirá después.

✓ Descubre qué hace la gente para resolver los problemas o alcanzar sus metas.

Breves consejos para leer una novela

✓ Lee el título y el nombre del autor.

✓ Explora cuántos capítulos hay.

✓ Al leer, fíjate en el escenario y el tiempo en que transcurre la historia.

✓ Fíjate en los personajes principales y en lo que hacen.

✓ Pon atención a los sucesos, problemas y conflictos de la trama.

✓ Descubre cómo se resuelven los problemas al final.

Breves consejos para leer un cuento de misterio

✓ Lee el título para saber de qué trata el misterio.

✓ Fíjate en los personajes que quieren resolver el misterio y por qué quieren hacerlo.

✓ Busca pistas para resolver el misterio.

✓ Fíjate en cómo el autor crea suspenso.

✓ Busca pistas para adivinar qué ocurrirá después.

✓ Descubre cómo se resuelve el misterio al final.

Breves consejos para leer ficción histórica

✓ Lee el título y el nombre del autor.

✓ Fíjate en qué momento y lugar de la historia ocurre el cuento.

✓ Lee el cuento. Imagina cómo vivía la gente en esa época.

✓ Observa cómo los personajes participan en acontecimientos históricos.

✓ Compara cómo se resolvían los problemas en el pasado y cómo se resuelven hoy en día.

Breves consejos para leer una obra de teatro

✓ Lee el título y el nombre del dramaturgo.

✓ Lee la lista de personajes al principio de la obra.

✓ Fíjate en dónde ocurre cada acto de la obra.

✓ Busca los nombres de los personajes antes de sus diálogos.

✓ Pon atención a las palabras que indican cómo hablan y se mueven los personajes.

Breves consejos para leer una novela gráfica

✓ Lee el título y el nombre del autor.

✓ Antes de comenzar a leer, revisa las ilustraciones, o parte gráfica de la novela.

✓ Lee lo que dicen los personajes en los globos de diálogo.

✓ Mire las ilustraciones para saber cómo se sienten los personajes.

✓ Lee las descripciones de lo que pasa en las cajas de texto.

✓ Para seguir la secuencia de la historia, lee de panel a panel.

GRADE 5: REPRODUCIBLE FICTION BOOKMARKS

Share these bookmarks with your students to remind them of some key features of different fiction genres/text types.

Quick Clues for Reading Realistic Fiction

✓ Read the title and the author's name.

✓ Look for characters who are as believable as real people.

✓ Note if the problems characters have and the actions they take to solve them seem truthful.

✓ Decide if the outcomes are reasonable. Think about whether this could happen in real life.

✓ Think about the ending and decide if it is satisfactory.

Quick Clues for Reading a Novel

✓ Read the title and the author's name. Learn about the story on the back cover or book jacket.

✓ Note the setting and the time frame the story covers as you read.

✓ Look for major and minor characters and their role in the story.

✓ Follow the sequence of events and conflicts in the plot. Note if there are subplots.

✓ Decide if conflicts are resolved in the end.

Quick Clues for Reading a Mystery

✓ Read the title for a clue to what the mystery is.

✓ Note the characters who want to solve the mystery and why.

✓ Note how suspense builds as characters look for clues.

✓ Look for clues that foreshadow what will happen next.

✓ Find out in the end if the mystery is solved as you thought or if the ending is a surprise.

Quick Clues for Reading Historical Fiction

✓ Read the title and the author's name.

✓ Note when and where in history the story takes place.

✓ Note people's clothing, food, and homes. See what kind of work they do.

✓ See how characters take part in historical events.

✓ Look for how the setting affects what happens to the characters.

Quick Clues for Reading Science Fiction

✓ Read the title and the author's name.

✓ Find out if the story happens in the future and on another planet.

✓ Note details of the world in which the characters live.

✓ Look for scientific ideas that influence the plot.

✓ Read to see how characters solve problems and conflicts in this world.

Quick Clues for Reading a Play

✓ Read the title.

✓ Find a list of characters in the beginning.

✓ Read each act or part of the play. Note where each act takes place.

✓ Look for the names of characters and the words they say.

✓ Look for words that tell you how the characters speak and move.

MARCADORES REPRODUCIBLES/GÉNERO FICCIÓN

Reparta estos marcadores entre sus alumnos para que recuerden algunas de las características del texto en el género ficción.

Breves consejos para leer ficción realista

✓ Lee el título y el nombre del autor.

✓ Busca personajes que parezcan a personas reales.

✓ Determina si los problemas que tienen los personajes y las decisiones que toman para resolverlos parecen verídicos.

✓ Decide si los resultados son razonables. Piensa en si esto podría ocurrir en la vida real.

✓ Piensa en el final y determina si es satisfactorio.

Breves consejos para leer una novela

✓ Lee el título y el nombre del autor. Lee la contraportada o sobrecubierta para aprender más del libro.

✓ Mientras lees, fíjate en el escenario y en el periodo de tiempo en el que ocurre la historia.

✓ Busca los personajes principales y secundarios y su papel en la historia.

✓ Sigue la secuencia de sucesos y los conflictos de la trama. Fíjate si hay historias secundarias.

✓ Decide si al final los conflictos se resuelven o no.

Breves consejos para leer un cuento de misterio

✓ Lee el título para saber de qué trata el misterio.

✓ Fíjate en los personajes que quieren resolver el misterio y por qué quieren hacerlo.

✓ Nota que hay más misterio a medida que los personajes buscan pistas.

✓ Busca pistas que predigan qué sucederá después.

✓ Al final, descubre si el misterio se resolvió como pensabas o si fue una sorpresa.

Breves consejos para leer ficción histórica

✓ Lee el título y el nombre del autor.

✓ Fíjate en cuándo y dónde ocurre la historia.

✓ Presta atención a la vestimenta, alimentos y viviendas de la gente. Fíjate en qué trabajan.

✓ Lee cómo los personajes participan en acontecimientos históricos.

✓ Nota cómo el escenario influye en lo que le ocurre a los personajes.

Breves consejos para leer ciencia ficción

✓ Lee el título y el nombre del autor.

✓ Averigua si la historia ocurre en el futuro o en otro planeta.

✓ Fíjate en los detalles del mundo en que viven los personajes.

✓ Busca ideas científicas que influyan en la trama.

✓ Al leer, descubre cómo los personajes resuelven problemas y conflictos en ese mundo.

Breves consejos para leer una obra de teatro

✓ Lee el título.

✓ Busca la lista de personajes al principio de la obra.

✓ Lee todos los actos o partes de la obra. Fíjate en dónde ocurre cada acto.

✓ Busca los nombres de los personajes y lo que dicen.

✓ Busca palabras que te indiquen cómo hablan y se mueven los personajes.

GRADE 6: REPRODUCIBLE FICTION BOOKMARKS

Share these bookmarks with your students to remind them of some key features of different fiction genres/text types.

Quick Clues for Reading a Graphic Novel

✓ Read the title and the author's name.

✓ Preview the pictures, or graphic part of the novel, before you start reading.

✓ Find characters' words in the speech balloons.

✓ Look for how characters feel in the illustrations.

✓ Find descriptions of what happens in the text boxes on the illustrations.

✓ Follow the story sequence by moving from panel to panel.

Quick Clues for Reading a Novel

✓ Read the title and the author's name. Learn about the story on the back cover or book jacket.

✓ Decide where and when the story takes place as you begin to read.

✓ Identify the major and minor characters and the problems or conflicts they have.

✓ Follow the rising action in the plot.

✓ Decide where the story climax is and what resolution follows at the end.

Quick Clues for Reading an Adventure

✓ Read the title and author's name.

✓ Note the setting for the story.

✓ Identify the major and minor characters and the problems or conflicts they have.

✓ Follow the plot to identify exciting, and often risky, situations.

✓ Note how conflicts are resolved.

Quick Clues for Reading Historical Fiction

✓ Read the title and the author's name.

✓ Note the historical setting for the story.

✓ Pay attention to details of clothing, food preparation, and transportation to get a sense of the time period.

✓ Note any names of real places and real people in history.

✓ Decide how the setting influences the plot and the characters' actions.

Quick Clues for Reading Science Fiction

✓ Read the title for clues to what the story is about.

✓ Decide what the setting is: another planet, a spaceship, and/or the future.

✓ Note how the setting is different from the world in which you live.

✓ Decide how science or futuristic technology influences the plot.

✓ Follow the plot to identify conflicts and how they are resolved in the end.

Quick Clues for Reading a Myth

✓ Read the title to learn who and what the story is about.

✓ Read the story to decide what natural event or human question might be explained.

✓ Identify the setting and the culture the myth comes from.

✓ Look for human characters who may interact with gods and goddesses or mythical creatures.

✓ Note how conflicts are resolved.

MARCADORES REPRODUCIBLES/GÉNERO FICCIÓN

Reparta estos marcadores entre sus alumnos para que recuerden algunas de las características del texto en el género ficción.

Breves consejos para leer una novela gráfica

✓ Lee el título y el nombre del autor.

✓ Antes de comenzar a leer, revisa las ilustraciones, o parte gráfica de la novela.

✓ Lee lo que dicen los personajes en los globos de diálogo.

✓ Mira las ilustraciones para saber cómo se sienten los personajes.

✓ Lee las descripciones de lo que pasa en las cajas de texto.

✓ Para seguir la secuencia de la historia, lee de panel a panel.

Breves consejos para leer una novela

✓ Lee el título y el nombre del autor. Lee la contraportada o sobrecubierta para aprender más sobre el libro.

✓ Mientras lees, fíjate en dónde y cuándo ocurre la historia.

✓ Identifica los personajes principales y secundarios y sus problemas o conflictos.

✓ Sigue el desarrollo de la acción en la trama.

✓ Decide cuál es el climax de la historia y cuál es la resolución final.

Breves consejos para leer un aventura

✓ Lee el título y el nombre del autor.

✓ Nota el lugar donde tiene lugar la historia.

✓ Identifica el personaje principal, el personaje secundario y los problemas que ambos tienen.

✓ Sigue la trama para identificar situaciones emocionantes o peligrosas.

✓ Nota cómo se resuelven los problemas o conflictos.

Breves consejos para leer ficción histórica

✓ Lee el título y el nombre del autor.

✓ Fíjate en el escenario histórico del cuento.

✓ Para entender la época, fíjate en detalles como la vestimenta, la preparación de los alimentos y los medios de transporte.

✓ Fíjate en los nombres de lugares y personas verdaderos en la historia.

✓ Decide cómo el ambiente influye en la trama y en las acciones de los personajes.

Breves consejos para leer ciencia ficción

✓ Lee el título para comprender de qué trata la historia.

✓ Identifica el escenario: otro planeta, una nave espacial y/o el futuro.

✓ Fíjate en las diferencias entre el escenario del cuento y el mundo en que vives.

✓ Decide cómo la ciencia o la tecnología futurista influye en la trama.

✓ Sigue la trama para identificar conflictos y cómo se resuelven al final.

Breves consejos para leer mitos

✓ Lee el título para que sepas sobre quién o qué trata la historia.

✓ Lee el cuento para identificar a qué evento natural o interrogante humano se le puede encontrar una explicación.

✓ Identifica el escenario y la cultura de la cual proviene el mito.

✓ Fíjate en personajes humanos que interactúen con dioses o personajes míticos.

✓ Presta atención a cómo se resuelven los conflictos.

REPRODUCIBLE INFORMATIONAL TEXT BOOKMARKS

Share these bookmarks with your students to remind them of some of the key features of informational text.

Quick Clues for Reading Informational Text

✓ Preview the piece.

✓ Read the title, introduction, and headings to discover the main ideas.

✓ Make a prediction about the subject of the piece.

✓ Pay special attention to bold-faced words and extra graphic features.

✓ Study the graphic aids and read the captions carefully.

Quick Clues for Reading Maps

✓ Read the map title.

✓ Find the symbols.

✓ Look at the map key. Read the labels.

✓ Find the map scale.

✓ Find the compass rose.

Quick Clues for Reading Primary Sources

✓ First, read the title.

✓ Preview the text to learn about the topic.

✓ Read the main article.

✓ Read the primary source material. Ask yourself, "How does this information add to what I know about the topic?"

Quick Clues for Reading Graphs

✓ Read the title of the graph.

✓ Think about the topic.

✓ Look at each part of the graph and read each label.

✓ Think about what information is being represented.

✓ Look at the labels. Think about what the numbers stand for.

✓ For line graphs, use your finger to trace from each dot to the side and the bottom.

Quick Clues for Reading Reference Sources

✓ Look up your topic in the table of contents or index.

✓ Preview the text.

✓ Use the special features as you read.

✓ Think about how the information from the source fits with what you know.

Quick Clues for Reading Magazine Articles

✓ Read the title, deck, and subheadings to learn the main ideas.

✓ Predict what the article will be about.

✓ Notice any special features.

✓ Pay attention to bold-faced words.

✓ Study the graphic aids and read the captions carefully.

MARCADORES REPRODUCIBLES/TEXTO INFORMATIVOS

Reparta estos marcadores entre sus alumnos para que recuerden algunas de las características del texto en el género de no ficción.

Breves consejos para leer textos informativos

✓ Hojea el artículo.

✓ Lee el título, la introducción y los encabezamientos para determinar la idea principal.

✓ Haz una predicción sobre el tema del artículo.

✓ Presta atención especial a las palabras en negrita u otras características sobresalientes.

✓ Observa las gráficas y lee los pies de grabado detenidamente.

Breves consejos para leer mapas

✓ Lee el título del mapa.

✓ Busca los símbolos del mapa.

✓ Observa la leyenda del mapa.

✓ Lee los rótulos.

✓ Busca la escala.

✓ Busca la rosa náutica.

Breves consejos para leer fuentes de información

✓ Primero, lee el título.

✓ Haz una lectura preliminar del texto para tener una idea del tema.

✓ Lee el artículo principal.

✓ Mientras lees, pregúntate qué nueva información has aprendido sobre el tema.

Breves consejos para leer gráficas

✓ Lee el título de la gráfica. Piensa sobre el tema.

✓ Observa cada sección de la gráfica y lee cada rótulo.

✓ Piensa en la información que se presenta en la gráfica.

✓ Observa los rótulos. Piensa en qué significan los números que aparecen.

✓ En las gráficas lineales, marca con el dedo las líneas que van de cada punto a las coordenadas.

Breves consejos para leer fuentes de referencia

✓ Busca el tema de interés en la tabla de contenido o en el índice.

✓ Haz una lectura preliminar del texto.

✓ A medida que leas, ten en cuenta características especiales.

✓ Analiza si la información que aparece en esta fuente es la que necesitas.

Breves consejos para leer artículos de revista

✓ Lee el título, la introducción y los subtítulos para determinar la idea principal.

✓ Haz una predicción sobre el tema del artículo.

✓ Observa cualquier característica especial.

✓ Presta atención a las palabras en negrita.

✓ Estudia las gráficas y lee los rótulos detenidamente.

TECHNOLOGY

Information on Guided Reading and how to implement it in your classroom is provided at **www.scholastic.com.** In addition, the site contains numerous teacher, student, and parent resources related to books in the Guided Reading Program. Use these resources for independent and group extension activities.

teacher resources

student activities

Scholastic Reading Counts! quizzes are available for all the titles in the Guided Reading Program. These quizzes can be used to monitor student comprehension and make decisions about each student's instructional needs.

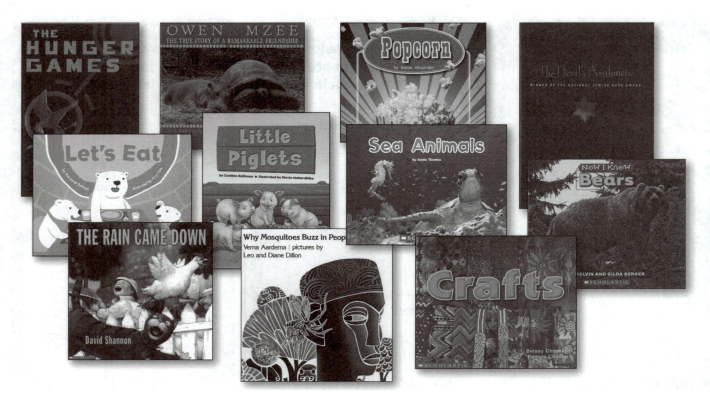

Skills & Strategies Chart

Level	Title	Author	Genre	Text Type	Themes	Comprehension Strategies	Phonics And Word Study	Writing Options	Technology
A	Butterfly	Jephson Gibbs	Fantasy	Picture Book	seeing the connection between butterflies and flowers; recognizing colors; learning about butterflies; using text and pictures to learn	Early Recognition of Punctuation	Initial Consonants	descriptive expository	http://www2.scholastic.com/browse/article.jsp?id=3746766 http://www.sandiegozoo.org/kids/craft_butterfly.html
A	Fruit Salad	Jephson Gibbs	Fantasy	Picture Book	eating healthful foods; working together; identifying different fruit; putting together a meal	Comparing and Contrasting	High-Frequency Words	label descriptive	http://www.mypyramid.gov/kids/index.html http://pbskids.org/zoom/activities/café
A	Let's Go!	Vanessa York	Fantasy	Picture Book	identifying ways to travel; traveling and going for a visit; having fun with family; seeing new places	Understanding Genre: Fantasy	Sentence Structure	expository label	http://www.atozkidstuff.com/tran.html http://www.nasa.gov/audience/for-students/k-4/stories/ames-how-planes-fly-slideshow.html
A	My Mom	Andy Greer	Realistic Fiction	Picture Book	participating in activities with family; having interests and hobbies; discovering that moms can be fun; learning how to do things	Developing Print Awareness	Action Words	poster narrative	http://www2.scholastic.com/browse/article.jsp?id=3749140 http://www.sproutonline.com/sprout/print/printasset.aspx?id=7918702б-1004-46ff-ac75-997a01819cdd
A	The Rabbit House	Bridie McBeath	Realistic Fiction	Picture Book	building a home for a pet; working together; learning what rabbits need; taking care of pets	Recognizing Sequence	Initial Sounds	descriptive narrative	http://www.humanesociety.org/animals/rabbits/tips/rabbits_as_pets.html http://www.pet-rabbit-care-information.com/best-pet.htm
A	Sea Animals	Annie Thomas	Informational Text	Picture Book	discovering animals in the sea; using text and pictures together to learn; noticing the wide variety of sea animals; seeing animals in their natural habitats	Using Photograph Details	Naming Words	fact sheet label	http://www.seaworld.org/animal-info/index.htm http://www.itsnature.org/category/sea/aquatic-mammals
A	The Store	Bridie McBeath	Informational Text	Picture Book	learning words for different clothing; identifying a store as a place to buy things; noticing details; following a theme	Activating Prior Knowledge	Words That Name More Than One	descriptive label	http://www.wisconsinhistory.org/museum/collections/online/pictsrch.cfm?ParentID=376566 http://pbskids.org/dontbuyit/advertisingtricks
A	The Three Frogs	Cynthia Rothman	Fantasy	Picture Book	having fun with music; performing as a team; recognizing patterns; identifying ways to move	Recognizing Patterned Text	Phonogram -op	label narrative	http://www.pca.state.mn.us/index.php/living-green/living-green-citizen/for-kids/frogs-for-kids.html www.sfkids.org/templates/instorchframe.asp?pageid=3
A	Time for Bed	Christina Master	Realistic Fiction	Picture Book	identifying bedtime routines; knowing the importance of sleep; feeling comfortable; enjoying your belongings	Recognizing Patterned Text	Pictures and Word Structure	narrative label	http://kidshealth.org/kid/stay_healthy/body/not_tired.html http://www2.scholastic. com/browse/parentsHome.jsp
A	Up!	Jane Craft	Fantasy	Series Book	solving a problem using one's abilities; understanding that different animals can move in different ways; working as a team; doing things differently	Recognizing Setting	Words With Short u	label list	http://www2.scholastic.com/browse/article.jsp?id=3746328 www.teachnology.com/worksheets/misc/back/rules/elem
B	Building Blocks	Alex Ives	Realistic Fiction	Picture Book	building something; using your imagination; playing with toys; recognizing how parts make a whole	Making Inferences	Telling Sentences	descriptive label	http://www.kidsource.com/education/building.mind.html http://www.bobthebuilder.com/usa/projects_playground.asp
B	Buster and Ziggy	Emily Clark	Fantasy	Picture Book	learning what dogs like to do; seeing how two pets get along; enjoying daily life; having things in common	Comparing and Contrasting	Words That Sound the Same	narrative label	http://www.akc.org/breeds/breeds_a.cfm http://pbskids.org/itsmylife/family/pets/article7.html
B	Color It Blue	Janet Reed	Informational Text	Picture Book	identifying the color blue; discovering the color blue in nature; identifying many shades of blue; studying photographs to comprehend text	Recognizing Story Pattern	High-Frequency Words	expository list	www.oregonzoo.org/Cards/Amazon/blue.poison.dart.frog.htm http://www.metmuseum.org/explore/learn_about_color/index.html
B	Hats	Sara Shapiro	Fantasy	Picture Book	identifying animal features; using descriptive words; using illustrations and text together for comprehension; recognizing your own features in others	Recognizing Story Pattern	Plurals	description expository	http://nationalzoo.si.edu/Animals/ http://www.pbs.org/wnet/nature/critter.html
B	My Cat	Annie Thomas	Realistic Fiction	Picture Book	identifying animal behaviors; spending time with a pet; knowing your pets' needs; observing a cat at play	Comparing and Contrasting	Action Words	expository list	http://animal.discovery.com/cat-guide/cat-behavior http://www.washingtonpost.com/wp-srv/kids/pets.htm
B	Party Time	Jane Craft	Fantasy	Series Book	celebrating a special occasion; spending time with friends; contributing to an event; having a picnic	Using Pictures	Initial Consonants	narrative expository	http://www2.scholastic.com/browse/search?query=parties http://store.scholastic.mn/webapp/wcs/stores/servlet/HomeView?storeId=1 0052&catalogId=10051
B	Polar Bears	Bailey Carroll	Informational Text	Picture Book	observing polar bear behavior; seeing animals in their natural habitat; seeing polar bears in action; using pictures to understand text	Understanding Photographs	Words With Short i	expository dialogue	http://www.bronxzoo.com/animals-and-exhibits/animals/mammals/polar-bear.aspx http://www.timeforkids.com/TFK/kids/news/story/0,28277,1984320,00.html
B	Puppy Paints	Cynthia Rothman	Fantasy	Picture Book	finding inspiration in the world around us; being creative; getting satisfaction from completing a job; having fun with paints	Reading Sentences	Action Words	list narrative	http://www.naturalchild.org/gallery http://pbskids.org/berenstainbears/art/coloring-act/index.html
B	School Fun	Stella Baker	Realistic Fiction	Picture Book	having fun at school; accomplishing things; learning new things; demonstrating skills	Making Predictions	Words With Consonants	narrative list	http://www2.scholastic.com/browse/article.jsp?id=4046 http://learnenglishkids.britishcouncil.org/language-games/paint-it
B	Where Is Bob?	Lindsay Winter	Realistic Fiction	Picture Book	seeking something that is lost; thinking of sensible places to look for something; finding the thing that makes you happy; loving your pet	Using Punctuation	Reading Contractions	narrative descriptive	http://www.aspca.org/pet-care/small-pet-care http://www.aspca.org/pet-care/small-pet-care/hamster-care.html
C	All Kinds of Pets	Michael Price	Realistic Fiction	Picture Book	visiting a pet shop; describing pet characteristics; making choices; making comparisons	Comparing and Contrasting	Describing Words	descriptive expository	http://www.bbc.co.uk/cbbc/wild/pets/goldfish.shtml http://www.mycitypets.com/do-birds-make-good-family-pets.html
C	Is It a Baby Animal?	Bridget Taylor	Informational Text	Picture Book	learning about baby animals; matching baby animals with their parents; observing details; comparing and contrasting	Recognizing Questions and Answers	Beginning and Ending Sounds	narrative expository	http://animal.discovery.com/guides/baby-animals/baby-animals.html http://www.umext.maine.edu/onlinepubs/htmpubs/2308.htm

Level	Title	Author	Genre	Text Type	Themes	Comprehension Strategies	Phonics And Word Study	Writing Options	Technology
C	**Let's Eat**	Margaret Bellings	Fantasy	Picture Book	helping set the table; working as a team; feeling satisfaction from a job well done; working towards a goal	Understanding Genre: Fantasy	Proper Nouns	graphic aid / list	http://www.chicagochildrensmuseum.org/learn_chores.html http://www.cyh.com/HealthTopics/HealthTopicDetailsKids.aspx?p=335&id=2526&np=287#
C	**Mrs. Cat Goes Shopping**	Vanessa York	Fantasy	Picture Book	solving problems; meeting one's needs; making decisions at the store; choosing healthful foods	Recognizing Sequence	Words With Short *a*	label / narrative	http://pbskids.org/arthur/games/supermarket/supermarket.html http://www.media-awareness.ca/english/games/coco/index.cfm
C	**My Costume**	Briar Wilton	Realistic Fiction	Picture Book	getting ready for a party; making choices; giving an opinion; having fun at a party	Recognizing Patterned Text	Punctuation	descriptive / graphic aid	http://familyfun.go.com/halloween/halloween-kids-costumes/ http://clubs-kids.scholastic.co.uk/clubs_assets/11566
C	**Pig Played**	Cynthia Rothman	Fantasy	Picture Book	having fun in different ways; solving a problem; getting ready for a bath; cleaning up after making a mess	Recognizing Setting	Short Vowels *i* and *u*	narrative / graphic aid	http://kidshealth.org/kid/talk/qa/wash_hands.html http://www.raisingspot.com/health-care/how-to-give-a-dog-bath
C	**Ready Freddy**	Cynthia Rothman	Realistic Fiction	Picture Book	getting ready to play in the snow; thinking ahead; dressing inappropriately; knowing the correct order in which to dress	Using Picture Details	Reading Punctuation	narrative / descriptive	http://www.cotf.edu/ete/modules/k4/weather/Whandson3.html http://www.utahtravelcenter.com/activities/skiing/
C	**The Sky**	Penelope Prince	Informational Text	Picture Book	observing the changing sky; noticing different kinds of weather; noticing how light affects the sky; seeing a rainbow	Using Picture Details	Describing Words	descriptive / narrative	http://eo.ucar.edu/webweather http://www.theweatherchannelkids.com
C	**Sleepy Bear**	Sara Mitchell	Fantasy	Picture Book	waking up for school; getting involved as a family; caring about family; passing of time	Using Punctuation	High-Frequency Words	list / letter	http://kidshealth.org/kid/stay_healthy/body/not_tired.html http://www.scholastic.com/kids/homework/calendar
C	**Under the Umbrella**	Jane Craft	Fantasy	Series Book	adapting to weather; identifying different animals and colors; identifying differences; selecting proper weather gear	Categorizing	Initial Sounds	label / narrative	http://www.weatherwizkids.com/ http://www.theweatherchannelkids.com/weather-ready/weatherready-guides/
D	**At the Toy Shop**	Libby Brereton	Fantasy	Picture Book	using your imagination; understanding action verbs; expecting the unexpected; playing with friends	Drawing Conclusions	Action Words	label / list	http://www2.scholastic.com/browse/article.jsp?id=10175 http://www.pbs.org/parents/tvschedules/
D	**The Band**	Libby Brereton	Fantasy	Picture Book	using your skills; working together; appreciating music; entertaining others	Distinguishing Fantasy From Reality	End Punctuation	label / narrative	http://www.dsokids.com/listen/instrumentlist.aspx http://www.spaghettibookclub.org/
D	**A Day at the Beach**	Kate Sinclair	Fantasy	Picture Book	gathering things to take to the beach; taking a family trip; helping each other; planning and preparing	Recognizing Patterned Text	Initial Consonant *t*	label / narrative	http://www.epa.gov/beaches/kids/about-beaches.html http://www.vbfun.com/visitors/articles/live_the_life_kid_style.aspx
D	**Farm Helpers**	Matt West	Realistic Fiction	Picture Book	using teamwork; the good feeling you get from a day's work; working as a family; sharing responsibilities	Recognizing Setting	Words With Long *e*	label / narrative	http://nationalzoo.si.edu/Animals/KidsFarm/default.cfm http://www2.scholastic.com/browse/article.jsp?id=3750050
D	**Ice Cream**	Briar Wilton	Fantasy	Picture Book	sharing with friends; being polite; enjoying a treat; misunderstanding a request	Recognizing Story Structure	Contractions	label / narrative	http://life.familyeducation.com/manners-and-values/parenting/34452.html http://pbskids.org/dontbuyit/advertisingtricks
D	**In the Desert**	Alex Ives	Informational Text	Picture Book	discovering the sights of the desert; using the senses for discovery; experiencing the beauty of nature; discovering desert plants and animals	Making Predictions	One- and Two-Syllable Words	label / narrative	http://www.desertmuseum.org/kids/oz/long-fact-sheets/ http://www.dbg.org/
D	**Little Piglets**	Cynthia Rothman	Fantasy	Picture Book	searching for something you want to find; recognizing farm animals; having perseverance; feeling relief when finding something that has been lost	Recognizing Patterned Text	Plurals	narrative / list	http://www.animalcorner.co.uk/farm/farm.html http://www.allkidsnetwork.com/crafts/animals/farm/pig-craft.asp
D	**Meet the Big Cats!**	Michael Stuart	Informational Text	Picture Book	learning about big cats; describing animals; distinguishing between different kinds of big cats; seeing animals in their habitats	Using Picture Details	Consonant Blends	expository / descriptive	http://nationalzoo.si.edu/Animals/PhotoGallery/GreatCats http://www.sandiegozoo.org/animalbytes/a-mammal.html
D	**Sand Animals**	Robert Harris	Realistic Fiction	Picture Book	making sand formations; competing can be fun; spending time with friends; using your imagination	Identifying Setting	Words With Short Vowels *e* and *a*	label / narrative	http://www.friendsofthedunes.org/news/sand_sculpture_festival/2008 http://www.epa.gov/sunwise/kids/index.html
D	**Who Is Getting Married?**	Bridie McBeath	Fantasy	Picture Book	celebrating a wedding; finding answers by asking questions; learning the names of animals; using the process of elimination	Recognizing Patterned Text	Words With Short *e*	list / graphic aid	http://parenting.leehansen.com/downloads/coloring/wedding/index.htm http://tlc.howstuffworks.com/family/greeting-cards5.htm/
E	**Bell**	Libby Brereton	Realistic Fiction	Series Book	not belonging to anyone; making a change; getting a new pet; taking care of yourself	Making Inferences	Short Vowel *u*	procedural / descriptive	http://www.catscans.com/facts.htm http://www.humanesociety.org/animals/cats/tips/cat_care_essentials.html
E	**Collections**	Margaret Ballinger and Rachel Gosset	Realistic Fiction	Picture Book	collecting things and keeping them safe; having hobbies; understanding labels; organizing your belongings	Activating Prior Knowledge	Compound Words	list / letter	http://www.smithsonianeducation.org/students/idealabs/amazing_collections.html http://www.usmint.gov/kids/campCoin/collectorsWorkshop/coinCourse/01.cfm
E	**Eat Your Peas, Louise!**	Pegeen Snow	Realistic Fiction	Picture Book	eating foods that are healthful; being polite is helpful; trying until you succeed; knowing what others like	Using Pictures	End Punctuation	recipe / label	http://www.nutritionexplorations.org/kids/nutrition-pyramid.asp http://kidshealth.org/kid/nutrition/food/breakfast.html
E	**Fish**	B. Lee Daniels	Informational Text	Picture Book	recognizing fish characteristics; seeing fish in natural habitats; understanding conservation; learning about life science	Recognizing Patterned Text	Short Vowel *i*	descriptive / label	http://www.montereybayaquarium.org/animals/AnimalList.aspx?a=Fishes http://www.jea.com/community/education/efficiency/wisely/save.html
E	**Fruit Trees**	B. Lee Daniels	Informational Text	Picture Book	learning how some fruit grows; learning that fruit is good for you; comparing shapes and colors; making healthful choices	Understanding Main Idea and Details	Consonant Blends	descriptive / list	http://www.pbhfoundation.org/educators/teachers/rainbow/ http://kidshealth.org/kid/recipes/recipes/fruit_kabobs.html
E	**I Love Rainy Days! (Noodles)**	Hans Wilhelm	Fantasy	Series Book	finding things to do indoors on a rainy day; being mischievous; realizing one person's fun can be another's problem; changing your mind	Understanding Cause and Effect	Words With Long *a*	label / narrative	http://library.sd.gov/forkids/rainyday.htm http://www.canismajor.com/dog/play1.html
E	**Let's Play in the Forest While the Wolf Is Not Around!**	Claudia Rueda	Fantasy	Picture Book	getting dressed; finding an unexpected twist; getting ready; playing with friends	Recognizing Story Structure	Words With *-ing*	descriptive / narrative	http://www.amnh.org/exhibitions/dioramas/wolf/ http://www.estcomp.ro/~cfg/games.html
E	**My New School**	Kirsten Hall	Realistic Fiction	Picture Book	going to a new school; learning important things at school; using spaces for different purposes; having fun at school	Setting	Action Words	caption / review	http://www2.scholastic.com/browse/search?query=new%20school http://www.wttw.com/main.taf?p=2,3

Level	Title	Author	Genre	Text Type	Themes	Comprehension Strategies	Phonics And Word Study	Writing Options	Technology
E	Ring! Ring!	Janelle Cherrington	Realistic Fiction	Picture Book	recognizing family communication; viewing family fun; identifying technology; recognizing animal behavior	Understanding Cause and Effect	Words With Digraphs	descriptive narrative	http://www.childdevelopmentinfo.com/parenting/manners.shtml http://www.fcc.gov/cgb/kidszone/faqs_k3.html
E	Sammy the Turtle	Amy Baker	Fantasy	Picture Book	knowing what you need to do; encouraging one another; trying until you succeed; working hard	Distinguishing Fantasy/Reality	Words With r-Controlled Vowels	list procedural	http://www2.scholastic.com/browse/article.jsp?id=11842 http://www.seaworld.org/infobooks/SeaTurtle/sthatch.html
F	Biscuit	Alyssa Satin Capucilli	Realistic Fiction	Series Book	taking care of a pet getting ready for bed; asking for things; putting off bedtime	Analyzing Character	Reading Punctuation	narrative descriptive	http://www.aspca.org/pet-care/dog-care/ http://www.whiskids.org/Lists/WithYourDog.htm
F	A Color of His Own	Leo Lionni	Fantasy	Picture Book	trying to change; accepting who you are; learning from others; making new friends	Reading Dialogue	Consonant Blends	riddle	http://www.sandiegozoo.org/animalbytes/t-chameleon.html http://www.spaghettibookclub.org/review.php?review_id=3735
F	A Day with Paramedics	Jan Kottke	Informational Text	Picture Book	learning about helping others; understanding the occupation of paramedic; recognizing the tools of a job; understanding informational text	Using Photographs	Unfamiliar Words	descriptive expository	http://kidshealth.org/kid/watch/house/emergency.html?tracking=K_RelatedArticle# http://www.kidsnewsroom.org/careers/careers.asp
F	Does a Kangaroo Have a Mother, Too?	Eric Carle	Informational Text	Picture Book	learning about animal families; understanding a mother's love; comparing animal and human families; learning animal names	Recognizing Sentence Pattern	Ending Consonants	expository letter	http://www.eric-carle.com/home.html http://www.sandiegozoo.org/animalbytes/index.html
F	Don't Be Late!	Libby Brereton	Realistic Fiction	Picture Book	being late; rushing to get ready on time; preparing for a trip; interacting with your family	Reading Everyday Speech	Exclamation Points	list narrative	http://www.time-for-time.com/ http://maps.google.com/
F	Little Bird	Libby Brereton	Fantasy	Picture Book	trying new things; getting lost; growing up; being helped by a parent	Making Inferences	Consonant Blends	expository descriptive	http://pbs.org/wnet/nature/lessons/bringing-up-birdy/video-segments-american-eagle/4762/ http://kidshealth.org/kid/exercise/fit/work_it_out.html
F	My River	Shari Halpern	Fantasy	Picture Book	living together in harmony; understanding a river habitat; studying ecology; recognizing that rivers are important	Understanding Genre: Fantasy	Words With Long i	narrative expository	http://www.nps.gov/miss/naturescience/animals.htm http://australianmuseum.net.au/Wild-Kids-Animals-of-freshwater-habitats
F	Popcorn	Karen Alexander	Informational Text	Picture Book	learning about how corn grows; learning what makes popcorn pop; learning about farm crops; using text and photos to learn	Making Inferences	Words That Describe	list recipe	http://www.popcorn.org/EncyclopediaPopcornica/tabid/57/Default.aspx http://www.fsa.usda.gov/FSA/kidsapp?area=home&subject=fun!&topic=landing
F	Small Treasures	Akimi Gibson	Realistic Fiction	Picture Book	using your imagination; treasuring items; enjoying playtime; recognizing what makes things special	Summarizing	Words With or	descriptive expository	www2.scholastic.com/browse/home.jsp http://www.sandiegozoo.org/kids/craft_caterpiller
F	Tina's Taxi	Betsy Franco	Realistic Fiction	Picture Book	going to work; following a routine; getting around; helping others	Recognizing Sequence of Events	Short Vowels	graphic aid narrative	http://www2.scholastic.com/wnet/taxidreams/panoramas/index.html http://www.ehow.com/how_5379423_make-car-shoe-box.html
G	Are We There Yet?	Bridget Taylor	Fantasy	Picture Book	feeling exhausted; taking a walk; spending time with family; growing impatient	Understanding Pat-terned Text	Dialogue	descriptive narrative	http://www.tpwd.state.tx.us/kids/get_out/hike.phtml http://www.nhs.uk/Change4Life/Pages/walk-for-life.aspx
G	A City Park	Jamie Barrow	Informational Text	Picture Book	ways to enjoy a city park; why city parks are special places; having fun with family and friends; recognizing parts of a community	Understanding Main Idea and Details	Reading Synonyms and Antonyms	graphic map expository	http://www.planning.org/cityparks/briefingpapers/helpchildrenlearn.htm http://www2.scholastic.com/browse/article.jsp?id=11401
G	Clifford Makes the Team	Norman Bridwell	Fantasy	Series Book	including everyone in play time; solving problems; learning about baseball; being a thoughtful friend	Understanding Character	Words With Short a	list letter	www.pbs.org/kenburns/baseball/beginners http://pbskids.org/zoom/activities/games/
G	Crafts	Betsey Chessen and Pamela Chanko	Informational Text	Picture Book	crafts from different cultures; making crafts; answering questions; appreciating other cultures	Using Picture Details	Question Sentences	descriptive procedural	http://www2.scholastic.com/browse/activities.jsp http://www.marthastewart.com/photogallery/kids-accessories
G	Lost and Found	Vanessa York	Realistic Fiction	Picture Book	finding a lost pet; making new friends; taking care of a pet; helping others	Understanding Plot	Dialogue	narrative list	http://www.humanesociety.org/animals/resources/tips/what_to_do_lost_pets.html http://www.examiner.com/dogs-in-memphis/what-to-do-if-you-find-a-lost-dog
G	Mousetrap	Diane Snowball	Fantasy	Picture Book	identifying different kinds of noises; escaping from danger; rooting for the underdog; having fun with sound words	Understanding Setting	Words With oo	description poetry	http://www.story-lovers.com/listsmousestories.html http://www.scholastic.com/readit/pdfs/FS.Geronimo.pdf
G	The New Car	Robert Lee	Realistic Fiction	Picture Book	the difficulties of making a decision; what people do before buying a car; looking at ads; replacing belongings	Comparing and Contrasting	Reading Action Words With -ed	expository graphic aid	http://americanhistory.si.edu/onthemove http://www.nhtsa.gov/people/injury/childps/PlayItSafeWeb/pages/GoodWaystoGoPlaces.htm
G	Our Tree House	Libby Brereton	Fantasy	Picture Book	sharing your possessions with others; joining a club; celebrating differences; having gatherings	Comparing and Contrasting	Consonant Blends	list narrative	http://animal.discovery.com/mammals/ http://www.studyzone.org/testprep/ela4/o/persuasivetechniquesL.cfm
G	Vegetable Soup	Ann Morris	Realistic Fiction	Picture Book	making vegetable soup; identifying different kinds of vegetables; following steps in order; enjoying a meal	Recognizing Sequence	Contractions	label list	http://www.kidsacookin.org http://www.sandiegozoo.org/kids/recipes_flamingo
G	Wake Up, Little Mouse!	Annie Thomas	Fantasy	Picture Book	being careful in dangerous situations; helping your family; facing danger; identifying problems between people and animals	Distinguishing Fantasy from Reality	Exclamatory Sentences	descriptive narrative	http://docs.schoolnutrition.org/meetingsandevents/nsbw2011 http://kidshealth.org/kid/stay_healthy/food/labels.html
H	Canada	Susan Canizares and Samantha Berger	Informational Text	Picture Book	learning about a different country; identifying diversity; comparing landscapes; recognizing people's traits	Noticing Details	Consonant Blends	expository persuasive	http://www.canadiangeographic.ca/kids/fun-facts/default.asp http://www.canadiangeographic.ca/kids/maps/default.asp
H	Captain Cat	Syd Hoff	Fantasy	Picture Book	recognizing military life; caring for loved ones; understanding one's responsibilities; taking care of pets	Recognizing Setting	Exclamatory Sentences	narrative list	http://www.psychologytoday.com/ http://www.petsandkids.co.uk/Cats.html
H	I Need a Lunch Box	Jeannette Caines	Realistic Fiction	Picture Book	getting ready for school; being eager to grow up; respecting parents; having hopes	Categorizing Information	Plurals	list note	http://kidshealth.org/kid/feeling/home_family/sibling_rivalry.html http://www.lunchboxes.com/fun.html

Level	Title	Author	Genre	Text Type	Themes	Comprehension Strategies	Phonics And Word Study	Writing Options	Technology
H	Inside Mouse, Outside Mouse	Lindsay Barrett George	Fantasy	Picture Book	contrasting the indoors and outdoors; observing the behavior of animals; meeting new friends; recognizing similarities	Comparing and Contrasting	Consonant Blends	descriptive, narrative	http://www.storyarts.org/library/aesops/stories/city.html http://www.ypte.org.uk/animal/mouse-harvest-/146
H	Just Me and My Dad (Little Critter)	Mercer Mayer	Fantasy	Series Book	having fun in the outdoors; engaging in an activity with a parent; experiencing an adventure; helping a parent	Using Picture Clues	Short Vowel Sounds	narrative, letter	http://kidshealth.org/kid/feeling/emotion/self_esteem.html http://www.gameskidsplay.net/games/mental_games/camping_trip.htm
H	Larry and Loki	Libby Brereton	Realistic Fiction	Picture Book	forgiving others; feeling guilty about mistakes; learning how to trust; getting in trouble	Making Predictions	Words That Name More Than One	narrative, rhyme	http://www.sspca.org/Cats http://drawsketch.about.com/library/bl-step-cat.htm
H	Mom's Secret	Meredith Costain	Realistic Fiction	Picture Book	sharing secrets; growing families; making guesses; having a surprise	Using Punctuation	Dialogue	descriptive, expository	http://pbskids.org/wayback/family/tree/index.html http://kidshealth.org/kid/feeling/home_family/new_baby.html
H	Now I Know: What's Under the Ocean?	Melvin and Gilda Berger	Informational Text	Picture Book	learning about ocean life; comparing living things; understanding animal habitats; learning more about earth	Comparing and Contrasting	Consonant Blends	descriptive, persuasive	http://www.nature.org/initiatives/marine/activities/ http://www.montereybayaquarium.org/animals/
H	The Story of Henny Penny	Retold by Richard Carson	Folktale	Picture Book	thinking things through; spreading rumors; communicating correctly; recognizing patterns in text	Recognizing Patterned Text	Recognizing Questions and Exclamations	narrative, list	http://teacher.scholastic.com/writewit/mff/index.htm http://www.mass.gov/rmv/mcmanual/20_TrafficSigns.pdf
H	Too Late Harry!	Sara Shapiro	Realistic Fiction	Picture Book	helping others; being late; building or cooking something; using specific tools for tasks	Monitoring Comprehension	Long a: Consonant + Final -e Pattern	list, expository	http://teacher.scholastic.com/scholasticnews/indepth/idolgiveback/pdfs/globalcitizenactivities.pdf http://kidshealth.org/kid/recipes/recipes/french_toast.html
I	The Birthday Party	Alex Ives	Realistic Fiction	Picture Book	celebrating special occasions; making preparations for special events; spending time with family; solving problems	Drawing Conclusions	Imperative Sentences	expository, descriptive	http://www2.scholastic.com/browse/article.jsp?id=3746786 http://emilypost.com/everyday-manners/table-manners/71-table-setting-guides
I	Dragon Gets By	Dav Pilkey	Fantasy	Series Book	getting mixed up; solving problems; enjoying life; being responsible	Understanding Sequence	Compound Words	narrative, letter	http://www.pilkey.com/books.php http://teamnutrition.usda.gov/resources/mpk_close.pdf
I	Henry and Mudge and the Funny Lunch	Cynthia Rylant	Realistic Fiction	Series Book	celebrating holidays; doing projects with family members; making a meal; being creative	Understanding Plot	Compound Words	expository, greeting card	http://www.kidsturncentral.com/holidays/glossary/holidaysgloss http://kidshealth.org/kid/recipes/index.html
I	Hi! Fly Guy	Tedd Arnold	Fantasy	Picture Book	having an unusual pet; continuing to persevere; defying expectations of others; finding value where others don't	Distinguishing Fantasy From Reality	Comparatives: -est	descriptive, narrative	http://insects.tamu.edu/fieldguide/cimg237.html http://www.avma.org/careforanimals/kidscorner/default.asp
I	Now I Know: Bears	Melvin and Gilda Berger	Informational Text	Picture Book	identifying different kinds of bears; understanding how cubs grow into bears; understanding how bears use camouflage; understanding hibernation	Comparing and Contrasting	Words With r-Controlled Vowels	descriptive, narrative	http://www.bears.org/animals http://www.nrdc.org/globalwarming/polaraction.pdf
I	Now I Know: Butterflies	Melvin and Gilda Berger	Informational Text	Picture Book	recognizing butterfly characteristics; learning about butterfly life cycles; learning about different butterfly types; using text features	Understanding Genre: Informational Text	Reading Punctuation	narrative, descriptive	http://www.naba.org/index.html http://crafts.kaboose.com/butterfly1.html
I	Small Pig	Arnold Lobel	Fantasy	Picture Book	dealing with change; leaving home; losing something important; feeling loved	Understanding Cause and Effect	Compound Words	descriptive, narrative	http://www.childcareaware.org/en/subscriptions/dailyparent/volume.php?id=34 http://www.nysgtsc.state.ny.us/Kids/kid-bike.htm
I	The Very Busy Spider	Eric Carle	Fantasy	Picture Book	watching a spider spin its web; recognizing farm animals; working hard gives rewards; discovering what spiders eat	Recognizing Story Structure	Initial Consonant Blends	descriptive, expository	http://www.amnh.org/sciencebulletins/biobulletin/biobulletin/story991.html http://www.ziggityzoom.com/activities.php?a=343
I	Who Wants a Ride?	Robin Bernard	Realistic Fiction	Picture Book	carrying baby animals; seeing animals in their natural habitats; learning about animal behavior; going places	Using Picture Clues	Action Words	narrative, expository	http://www.kangarooworlds.com/ http://www.zooborns.com/zooborns/baby-animal-names.html
I	Willie's Wonderful Pet	Mel Cebulash	Realistic Fiction	Picture Book	joining in class activities; being a creative problem solver; working and playing with friends; having confidence	Understanding Sequence	Dialogue	label/caption, descriptive	http://pbskids.org/itsmylife/family/pets/article4.html http://pbskids.org/itsmylife/family/pets/article7.html
J	Dig Dig Digging	Margaret Mayo	Informational Text	Picture Book	using machines for work; operating heavy equipment; building and repairing things; using descriptive details	Understanding Genre: Informational Text	Words With -ing	expository, graphic aid	http://science.howstuffworks.com/transport/engines-equipment/fire-engine.htm http://www2.scholastic.com/browse/article.jsp?id=11739
J	Have You Seen Duck?	Janet A. Holmes and Jonathan Bentley	Realistic Fiction	Picture Book	having a best friend; coping with loss; having a favorite toy; searching for something that is lost	Understanding Character	Dialogue	narrative, descriptive	http://charityguide.org/volunteer/fifteen/donate-toys.htm http://www2.scholastic.com/browse/article.jsp?id=3754335
J	Henry and Mudge and the Best Day of All	Cynthia Rylant	Realistic Fiction	Series Book	enjoying the good things in life; having a dog as a best friend; spending time with friends; celebrating a birthday	Making Inferences	Reading Compound Words	narrative, letter	http://www2.scholastic.com/browse/article.jsp?id=549 http://www2.scholastic.com/browse/search?query=o5%20so%20cute
J	Hippo and Rabbit in Three Short Tales	Jeff Mack	Fantasy	Short Stories	playing with a friend; sharing with another; helping a friend; being scared at bedtime	Drawing Conclusions	Homophones	narrative, descriptive	http://www2.scholastic.com/browse/article.jsp?id=3666 http://pbskids.org/arthur/firesafety/index.html
J	I Was So Mad (Little Critter)	Mercer Mayer	Fantasy	Series Book	overcoming frustration; adapting to changes in mood; exhibiting emotion; wanting to do what you cannot	Understanding Cause and Effect	Contractions	narrative, list	http://kidshealth.org/kid/feeling/emotion/anger.html http://www.printablesigns.net
J	Log Hotel	Anne Schreiber	Informational Text	Picture Book	exploring the life cycle of a tree; describing changes in nature; identifying natural resources; exploring plant and animal habitats	Understanding Sequence	Words With r-Controlled Vowels	expository, persuasive	http://ogdennaturecenter.org/education/37/100-trees-tree-life-cycle http://cms.ran.org/new/kidscorner/kid_s_action/letters_from_kids_to_companies

Level	Title	Author	Genre	Text Type	Themes	Comprehension Strategies	Phonics And Word Study	Writing Options	Technology
J	**The Rain Came Down**	David Shannon	Realistic Fiction	Picture Book	getting caught in a chain reaction; how surroundings impact outlook; how the moods of others affect us; individuals having feelings that are common to all people	Identifying Cause and Effect	Words With -ed	descriptive expository	http://eo.ucar.edu/webweather http://www.weather.gov
J	**Story County**	Derek Anderson	Fantasy	Picture Book	working together; finding ways to be creative; following a plan; identifying things on a farm	Recognizing Story Sequence	Dialogue	list narrative	http://www.emints.org/ethemes/resources/S00001819.shtml http://www.bbc.co.uk/cbeebies/#/fb/comeoutside/downonthefarm
J	**The Wrong-way Rabbit**	Teddy Slater	Fantasy	Chapter Book	doing things in an individual way; going against the flow; fitting in with others; being creative	Using Illustrations	Using Punctuation	narrative persuasive	http://kidshealth.org/parent/positive/talk/tolerance.html http://www.nysgtsc.state.ny.us/Kids/kidswalk.htm
J	**Young Cam Jansen and the Baseball Mystery**	David A. Adler	Mystery	Series Book	solving a mystery; admitting our mistakes; paying attention to details; drawing conclusions	Generating Questions	Understanding Contractions	persuasive expository	http://www.camjansen.com/index.htm http://www.exploratorium.edu/memory/dont_forget/index.html
K	**10 Fat Turkeys**	Tony Johnston	Fantasy	Picture Book	counting down from ten; getting into mischief; enjoying silly humor; using rhyme and onomatopoeia	Using Illustrations	Long i: Consonant + Final e Pattern	descriptive poetry	http://www.acpl.lib.in.us/children/counting.html http://www.citypl.com/police/kid_safety_skating.html
K	**Andy Shane and the Queen of Egypt**	Jennifer Richard Jacobson	Realistic Fiction	Series Book	finding ways to work together; forgiving your friends; accepting help; appreciating other cultures	Understanding Character	Multiple-Meaning Words	graphic aid narrative	http://www.mfa.org/egypt/explore_ancient_egypt/index.html http://www.egyptvacation.com/?source=google
K	**Arthur's Eyes (An Arthur Adventure)**	Marc Brown	Fantasy	Series Book	accepting yourself as you are; dealing with teasing; solving problems; getting eyeglasses	Understanding Cause and Effect	Contractions	journal narrative	http://www.lehman.cuny.edu/faculty/jfleitas/bandaides/teasetips.html http://kidshealth.org/kid/htbw/eyes.html
K	**Chicks and Salsa**	Aaron Reynolds	Fantasy	Picture Book	trying something new; living on a farm; following recipes; finding humor in illustrations	Understanding Setting	Subject-Area Words	descriptive poetry	http://teacher.scholastic.com/scholasticnews/indepth/one_world/lesson_plans/lesson.asp?article=lesson5 http://www.fda.gov/food/labelingnutrition/consumerinformation/ucm078889.htm
K	**Dandelions: Stars in the Grass**	Mia Posada	Informational Text	Picture Book	understanding the life cycle of a plant; finding beauty in surroundings; appreciating the processes that occur in nature; examining an everyday sight more carefully	Recognizing Sequence	Plurals	descriptive narrative	http://plants.usda.gov/java/profile?symbol=TAOF http://www.sandiegozoo.org/kids/recipes.html
K	**Earl the Squirrel**	Don Freeman	Fantasy	Picture Book	learning to be self-reliant; being appreciative of others' help; growing up; helping a friend	Understanding Plot	The Suffix -ly	narrative letter	http://www.backyardnature.com/cgi-bin/gt/tpl.h,content=501 http://www.metmuseum.org/explore/FUN/artgame1.html
K	**Endangered Animals**	Faith McNulty	Informational Text	Picture Book	protecting endangered species; understanding the balance of nature; identifying endangered animals; identifying environmental issues	Understanding Cause and Effect	Plurals	expository persuasive	http://www.kidsplanet.org http://www.savethepolarbear.org
K	**Frog and Toad All Year**	Arnold Lobel	Fantasy	Short Stories	spending time with friends; enjoying things in each season; making discoveries; helping friends	Summarizing	Irregular Past-Tense Verbs	expository list	http://www2.scholastic.com/browse/contributor.jsp?id=3077 http://www.starfall.com/n/holiday/calendar/load.htm?f
K	**One Nosy Pup**	Carol Wallace	Fantasy	Chapter Book	making new friends; solving problems; helping those you care about; caring for pets responsibly	Understanding Problems and Solutions	Multisyllabic Words	narrative label	http://www.mspca.org/programs/pet-owner-resources http://www.humanesociety.org/animals/hamsters/tips/hamster_tips.html
K	**The Principal From the Black Lagoon**	Mike Thaler	Fantasy	Series Book	letting one's fears take hold; letting one's imagination run wild; respecting others; discerning between reality and fantasy	Recognizing Point of View	Compound Words	descriptive expository	http://www2.scholastic.com/browse/contributor.jsp?id=3686http://newspaperforkids.com
L	**Amelia Bedelia, Rocket Scientist?**	Herman Parish	Realistic Fiction	Series Book	misunderstanding words and ideas; working together; dealing with confusion; solving problems	Understanding Cause and Effect	Multiple-Meaning Words	expository descriptive	http://www2.scholastic.com/browse/lessonplan.jsp?id=902 http://kidshealth.org/kid/recipes/recipes/pineapple_pops.html
L	**Cam Jansen and the Chocolate Fudge Mystery**	David A. Adler	Mystery	Series Book	questioning first impressions; solving problems; being persistent; breaking rules	Problem and Solution	Compound Words	persuasive descriptive	http://www.davidaadler.com http://www.savethewhales.org/adopt.html
L	**Let's Read About ... George Washington**	Kimberly Weinberger	Biography	Picture Book	leading a nation; making a difference; serving one's country; fighting for a cause	Understanding Historical Context	Names for People and Places	letter expository	http://www.whitehouse.gov/about/presidents/georgewashington http://www.pbs.org/georgewashington/timeline/index.html
L	**Our Earth**	Anne Rockwell	Informational Text	Picture Book	understanding geography; learning about earth; comparing and contrasting; learning about different land forms	Noticing Details	Reading Words with -y and -ly	expository descriptive	http://spaceplace.nasa.gov/en/kids/srtm_make1.shtml http://www.timeforkids.com/TFK/media/hh/pdfs/samplepapers/persuasive_sample.pdf
L	**Ricky Ricotta's Mighty Robot vs. the Uranium Unicorns From Uranus**	Dav Pilkey	Science Fiction	Series Book	surviving many challenges; triumphing over evil; supporting friends; facing challenges	Making Predictions	Reading Words With -ed	descriptive narrative	http://www.scholastic.com/titles/rickyricotta/index.htm http://kids.niehs.nih.gov/recycle.htm
L	**Stand Tall, Molly Lou Melon**	Patty Lovell	Fantasy	Picture Book	being proud of who you are; coping with people and events; dealing with bullies; making friends	Understanding Theme	Comparatives -er and -est	descriptive list	http://www.education.com/magazine/article/Helping_Children_Make_Friends/ http://www.marthastewart.com/article/decorating-with-paper-snowflakes
L	**The Subway Mouse**	Barbara Reid	Fantasy	Picture Book	facing the unknown; following your dreams despite difficult conditions; making a connection with someone who supports you; letting stories inspire you	Understanding Problem and Solution	Contractions	expository narrative	http://teacher.scholastic.com/activities/immigration/index.htm http://www.nps.gov/isro/planyourvisit/upload/Safety%20Tips%20for%20Hiking-2.pdf
L	**Tony Baloney**	Pam Munoz Ryan	Fantasy	Picture Book	using your imagination; finding your place in a large family; getting along with others; acting out for attention	Using Illustrations	Understanding Idioms	narrative descriptive	http://www.pammunozryan.com/index.html http://www.nysgtsc.state.ny.us/Kids/kid-schl.htm
L	**Whales Passing**	Eve Bunting	Realistic Fiction	Picture Book	appreciating nature; recognizing animal behavior; observing wildlife; spending time with loved ones	Recognizing Point of View	Homophones	descriptive narrative	http://www.kidsplanet.org/factsheets/orca.html http://www.sheddaquarium.org/explore_by_animal.html
L	**Worms for Lunch?**	Leonid Gore	Fantasy	Picture Book	learning about animals; identifying what animals eat; contrasting food habits; exploring different ways of eating	Understanding Genre: Fantasy	Synonyms	list narrative	http://nationalzoo.si.edu/Animals/AnimalIndex/AnimalNews/nutrition.cfm http://www.marthastewart.com/cooking-with-kids

Level	Title	Author	Genre	Text Type	Themes	Comprehension Strategies	Phonics And Word Study	Writing Options	Technology
M	**Baby Animals**	Melvin and Gilda Berger	Informational Text	Picture Book	amazing facts about familiar and not so familiar baby animals; distinguishing between true and false; comparing and contrasting baby and grown up animals; how animals care for their young	Visualizing	Context Clues	descriptive; persuasive	http://www.denverzoo.org/animals/mammals.asp http://pbskids.org/zoom/activities/sci/birdfeeder.html
M	**The Case of the Groaning Ghost (A Jigsaw Jones Mystery)**	James Preller	Mystery	Series Book	solving mysteries by sticking to the facts; jumping to conclusions; working with others; reevaluating situations	Drawing Conclusions	Words With -ed	narrative; list	http://www.kidsloveamystery.com http://www2.scholastic.com/browse/lessonplan.jsp?id=446
M	**Class President (Marvin Redpost)**	Louis Sachar	Realistic Fiction	Series Book	dealing with the unexpected; feeling nervous in a classroom setting; understanding citizenship; interacting with a significant figure	Understanding Character	Words With Hard and Soft c	list; narrative	http://www.louissachar.com/Marvin.htm http://www.scholastic.com/kids/stacks/books/?lt=stacks/nav/books_and_authors
M	**Flat Stanley**	Jeff Brown	Fantasy	Series Book	dealing with change; appreciating our differences; appreciating the good ideas of others; using our unique qualities to benefit others	Distinguishing Fantasy From Reality	Comparatives: -er, -est	narrative; list	http://www.flatstanleybooks.com/teachers.aspx http://www.timeforkids.com/TFK/media/hh/pdfs/samplepapers/news_sample.pdf
M	**Goldilocks and the Three Bears**	Retold by James Marshall	Folktale	Series Book	respecting the property of others; understanding the importance of rules; learning from mistakes; respecting parents and guardians	Recognizing Sequence	Antonyms	letter; narrative	http://ivyjoy.com/fables/goldilocks.html http://www.nhtsa.gov/people/injury/childps/PlayItSafeWeb/pages/RuleoftheRoad.htm
M	**The Lamb Who Came for Dinner**	Steve Smallman	Fantasy	Picture Book	discovering friendship in an unusual setting; allowing ourselves to change our thinking; feeling sympathy for others; observing how the positive characteristics of one person can affect another	Understanding Cause and Effect	Figurative Language: Onomatopoeia	descriptive; narrative	http://library.thinkquest.org/03oct/00343/fairytaleindex.htm http://www.cookingwithkids.com/pep/soup/veg.html
M	**Miss Smith's Incredible Storybook**	Michael Garland	Fantasy	Series Book	the adventures reading can bring; figuring out a solution to a problem; unleashing imagination; chaos	Understanding Genre: Fantasy	Words With Long o	narrative; persuasive	http://www.garlandpicturebooks.com/garlandpicturebooks.com/Home.html http://www.honoluluzoo.org/komodo_dragon.htm
M	**No Messin' with My Lesson (Katie Kazoo, Switcheroo)**	Nancy Krulik	Fantasy	Series Book	walking in someone else's shoes; being honest with others; demonstrating appropriate behavior in the classroom; finding a solution to a problem	Making Inferences	Multisyllabic Words	list; narrative	http://pbskids.org/stantonanthony/day_in_life.html http://pbskids.org/itsmylife/advice/index.html
M	**Oh No, It's Robert**	Barbara Seuling	Realistic Fiction	Series Book	working towards a goal; helping others; trusting a friend; setting goals	Making Predictions	Possessive Words With 's	expository; letter	http://www2.scholastic.com/browse/article.jsp?id=3745989 http://www.kidsreads.com/features/more-features.asp
M	**Who Eats What? Food Chains and Food Webs**	Patricia Lauber	Informational Text	Picture Book	exploring food chains and food webs; exploring food sources; understanding the interdependence of all living things; identifying cause and effect relationships	Understanding Sequence	Compound Words	graphic aid; expository	http://www.cnr.berkeley.edu/citybugs/teachercorner/foodwebs.html http://www.ecokids.ca/pub/eco_info/topics/frogs/chain_reaction/play_chain-reaction.cfm
N	**Blizzard of the Blue Moon (Magic Tree House)**	Mary Pope Osborne	Fantasy	Series Book	working together to solve a mystery; exploring an unfamiliar place; seeking adventure; exploring a new historical context	Understanding Plot	Recognizing Contractions	graphic aid; poetry	http://www.centralpark.com/pages/maps.html http://www.fodors.com
N	**Brand-new School, Brave New Ruby (Ruby and the Booker Boys)**	Derrick Barnes	Realistic Fiction	Series Book	trying to fit in at a new school; stepping out of an older sibling's shadow; being unique, standing out; special talents	Understanding Sequence	Reading Compound Words	descriptive; list	http://www2.scholastic.com/browse/article.jsp?id=4377 http://www.scholastic.com/titles/deardumbdiary/game/diary.htm
N	**Detective LaRue: Letters from the Investigation**	Mark Teague	Fantasy	Series Book	distinguishing fantasy from reality; viewing different retellings of an event; creating fabrications to portray oneself differently; finding humor in an unfortunate situation	Making Inferences	Reading Words With Suffix -ly	letter; narrative	http://www.petuniversity.com/cats/behavior/cats-and-dogs.htm http://www.readwritethink.org/files/resources/interactives/letter_generator
N	**I Lost My Tooth in Africa**	Penda Diakité	Realistic Fiction	Picture Book	learning about other cultures; relating to people of different backgrounds; learning traditions in other cultures; exploring everyday life in another country	Understanding Sequence	Using a Pronunciation Guide	descriptive; narrative	http://travel.nationalgeographic.com/travel/countries/mali-guide http://kids.nationalgeographic.com/kids/places
N	**Lunch Walks Among Us (Franny K. Stein, Mad Scientist)**	Jim Benton	Science Fiction	Series Book	being true to yourself; appreciating the differences between people; accepting people for what they are; wanting to fit in	Using Picture Words	Difficult Words	expository; descriptive	http://kidshealth.org/kid/feeling/friend/make_friends.html http://www.omsi.edu/flubber
N	**The Phantom Mudder (Jack Russell: Dog Detective)**	Darrel and Sally Odgers	Mystery	Series Book	solving a mystery; looking for clues; drawing conclusions; competing in a contest	Understanding Point of View	Suffixes -ion, -sion, and -tion	descriptive; narrative	http://www.westminsterkennelclub.org http://www.scholastic.com/bookfairs/contest/kaa_howtoenter.asp
N	**Sacajawea: Her True Story**	Joyce Milton	Biography	Picture Book	showing courage; assisting the Lewis and Clark expedition; learning about Native American history; learning about famous women in U.S. history	Generating Questions	Using a Punctuation Guide	letter; descriptive	http://www.monticello.org/jefferson/lewisandclark/origins.html http://www.pbs.org/lewisandclark/inside/saca.html
N	**Why Mosquitoes Buzz in People's Ears**	Verna Aardema	Folktale	Picture Book	misunderstandings cause problems; getting to the bottom of a problem; following a chain reaction; identifying animals	Understanding Cause and Effect	Synonyms	descriptive; label	http://www.acpl.lib.in.us/children/howandwhy.html http://pbskids.org/africa/mask/hunter.html
N	**You Can't Eat Your Chicken Pox, Amber Brown**	Paula Danziger	Realistic Fiction	Series Book	making the best of a situation; finding out what makes you feel better; dealing with parental separation; preparing for the unexpected	Making Predictions	Multisyllabic Words with Consonant Clusters	letter; persuasive	http://www.bookpage.com/9602bp/childrens/pauladanziger.html http://kids.yahoo.com/games/game/imaginalis_anagrams
N	**Young Frederick Douglass: Freedom Fighter**	Andrew Woods	Biography	Picture Book	fighting for freedom; using your skills and talents to help others; using reading, writing, and speaking to change the world; not giving up on a goal	Setting	Words With -ed	expository; letter	http://www.pbs.org/wgbh/aia/part4/4p1539.html http://www.recycleworks.org/kids/index.html
O	**Amelia Earhart: Adventure in the Sky**	Francene Sabin and Joanne Mattern	Biography	Chapter Book	having the courage and spirit to follow one's dreams; defying stereotypes; overcoming assumptions; having the courage to make one's own path and decisions	Understanding Genre: Biography	Words With Suffixes	expository; narrative	http://www.americaslibrary.gov/aa/earhart/aa_earhart_subj.html http://maps4kids.com

Level	Title	Author	Genre	Text Type	Themes	Comprehension Strategies	Phonics And Word Study	Writing Options	Technology
O	Anansi Does the Impossible! An Ashanti Tale	Verna Aardema	Folktale	Picture Book	understanding common themes in folktales; finding creative ways to succeed; outsmarting another to win; understanding cleverness and trickery	Distinguishing Fantasy From Reality	r-Controlled Vowel Sound /or/	descriptive / letter	http://www.historyforkids.org/learn/africa/literature/anansi.htm http://www.kyv1.org/kids/glossary.html
O	Clementine	Sara Pennypacker	Realistic Fiction	Series Book	causing trouble without intent; solving problems in creative ways; being different; surviving bad days	Drawing Conclusions	Words with Soft c and Hard c	letter / narrative	http://www.sarapennypacker.com http://www.learner.org/workshops/middlewriting/images/pdf/jw-ice%20rink.pdf
O	John Philip Duck	Patricia Polacco	Realistic Fiction	Picture Book	reaping the rewards of hard work and determination; finding your own hidden talents; learning about John Philip Sousa; learning about marches	Understanding Problems and Solutions	Reading Words with -ed	expository / list	http://www.dws.org/sousa/works.htm http://www.peabodymemphis.com/peabody_ducks
O	Journey to the Volcano Palace (The Secrets of Droon)	Tony Abbott	Fantasy	Series Book	going on a journey; exploring a magical world; working with others to achieve a goal; fighting against evil	Making Predictions	Similes	descriptive / narrative	http://www.fema.gov/kids/volcano.htm http://www.tonyabbottbooks.com
O	A Mouse Called Wolf	Dick King-Smith	Fantasy	Chapter Book	developing an unlikely friendship; discovering the joy in music; realizing one's talents; accomplishing a goal	Understanding Cause and Effect	Diphthongs ou, ow	narrative / letter	http://teacher.scholastic.com/products/instructor/Jan05_music.htm http://www.sphinxkids.org/Composers_Gallery.html
O	Otis Spofford	Beverly Cleary	Realistic Fiction	Chapter Book	understanding the consequences of actions; standing up for yourself; finding humor in everyday things; discovering people are not what they seem	Understanding Character	Recognizing Adverbs	expository / narrative	http://www.beverlycleary.com http://healthiergeneration.org/schools.aspx?id=3312
O	Teacher's Pet (Jake Drake)	Andrew Clements	Realistic Fiction	Series Book	showing favoritism; being a good citizen and student; dealing with peer pressure; standing up for yourself	Understanding Plot	Comparatives: -er, -est	descriptive / expository	http://www.andrewclements.com http://kidshealth.org/kid/feeling/school/getting_along_teachers.html#
O	What's the Big Idea, Ben Franklin?	Jean Fritz	Biography	Picture Book	understanding an inventor's drive; using one's interests to benefit others; exploring characteristics of a famous figure; understanding historical events	Categorizing Information	Multisyllabic Words	expository / graphic aid	http://www.ushistory.org/franklin/ http://www.worldalmanac.com/world-almanac-kids.aspx
O	You Can't Taste a Pickle With Your Ear	Harriet Ziefert	Informational Text	Picture Book	experiencing the world by using the five senses; how each sense works; understanding animals' senses; how the brain helps senses work	Summarizing	Comparatives: -er, -est	expository / list	http://faculty.washington.edu/chudler/introb.html#se http://www.gigglepoetry.com/poetryclass.aspx
P	97 Ways to Train a Dragon (Dragon Slayers' Academy)	Kate McMullan	Fantasy	Series Book	treatment of animals; responsibility of caring for another; breaking the rules; keeping secrets	Understanding Problems and Solutions	Vivid Verbs	expository / narrative	www.amnh.org/exhibitions/mythiccreatures/dragons www.humanesociety.org/animals/dogs/tips/dog_training_positive_reinforcement.html
P	Copper	Kazu Kibuishi	Fantasy	Graphic Novel	using your imagination; exploring fantastical places; facing fears; being a friend	Understanding Text Structure	Onomatopoeia	descriptive / narrative	http://www.boltcity.com/workshop/copper_tutorial/ http://www.kidsreads.com/reviews/9780545098939.asp
P	Gooseberry Park	Cynthia Rylant	Fantasy	Chapter Book	going to great lengths for a friend; finding friendship in unlikely places; being faithful and true to friends; keeping an open mind	Summarizing	Compound Words	descriptive / expository	http://www.cyh.com/HealthTopics/HealthTopicDetailsKids.aspx?p=335&np=286&id=1636 http://www.missingpetpartnership.org/recovery-posters.php
P	Happy Burger	Chuck Ranberg and Patrick Daley	Realistic Fiction	Play	making the most with what you have been given; working hard for something you want; finding good in something bad; learning the value of a real friendship	Making Predictions	Words With Suffix -ly	descriptive / persuasive	http://www.kids.gov/k_5/k_5_careers.shtml http://www.scholastic.com/staysmart/pdf/g7_d20_reading.pdf
P	The Hunterman and the Crocodile	Baba Wagué Diakité	Folktale	Picture Book	understanding right and wrong; valuing the earth; making compromises; respecting others	Recognizing Sequence	Onomatopoeia	narrative / expository	http://teacher.scholastic.com/writewit/mff/folktalewshop_index.htm http://www.gogreeninitiative.org/content/WhyGoGreen/
P	Knights of the Kitchen Table (The Time Warp Trio)	Jon Scieszka	Adventure	Series Book	using brains instead of brawn; being careful what you wish for; having an adventure; traveling through time	Making Inferences	Adverbs	narrative / persuasive	http://www.kingarthursknights.com/ http://www.historyforkids.org/learn/medieval/literature/roundtable.htm
P	Kooks in the Cafeteria (Comic Guy)	Timothy Roland	Realistic Fiction	Series Book	finding humor in disagreeable situations; writing comic strips; working at a school; having a close friend	Understanding Comic Strips	Figurative Language: Similes	narrative / expository	http://teacher.scholastic.com/writeit/humor/teacher/humorwriting.htm http://www.activitytv.com/511-number-toon-bat-and-baseball
P	The Magic School Bus Explores the Senses	Joanna Cole	Informational Text	Series Book	learning about the senses; having an adventure; preparing for a performance; taking a field trip	Using Diagrams	Multisyllabic Words	expository / narrative	http://www.scholastic.com/magicschoolbus/games/experiments/index.htm http://www.scholastic.com/kids/homework/todo.htm
P	My First Book of Biographies: Great Men and Women Every Child Should Know	Jean Marzollo	Biography	Picture Book	making the world a better place; working hard to accomplish goals; growing up to be a powerful adult; learning about famous people of the past	Understanding Biography	Context Clues	biography / procedural	http://www.americaslibrary.gov/aa/index.php http://library.thinkquest.org/J001156/forms%20of%20writing/formwriting.htm
P	Tar Beach	Faith Ringgold	Fantasy	Picture Book	setting imagination free; learning about African-American culture; dreaming about the future; feeling close to family	Using Picture Details	Figurative Language	descriptive / letter	http://www2.scholastic.com/browse/contributor.jsp?id=3566 www.craftsforkids.com/projects/tree_of_life.htm
Q	All About Manatees	Jim Arnosky	Informational Text	Picture Book	understanding manatee traits; recognizing people's effects on manatees; coexisting peacefully; having respect for nature	Understanding Comic Strips	Context Clues	descriptive / persuasive	http://www.defenders.org/wildlife_and_habitat/wildlife/manatee.php http://www.factmonster.com/atlas/
Q	Book Two: The Stonekeeper's Curse (Amulet)	Kazu Kibuishi	Fantasy	Graphic Novel	recognizing the dangers of power; understanding one's destiny; recognizing the struggle between good and evil; putting others before oneself	Drawing Conclusions	Understanding Idioms	graphic aid / descriptive	http://www.scholastic.com/amulet/ http://www.si.edu/encyclopedia_si/history_and_culture/Advertising_History.htm
Q	The Clue at the Bottom of the Lake (Cabin Creek Mysteries)	Kristiana Gregory	Mystery	Series Book	solving a mystery; solving problems; working as a team; gathering information	Understanding Problem/Solution	Compound Words	graphic aid / narrative	http://www2.scholastic.com/browse/unitplan.jsp?id=241+J119 http://www.mywonderfulworld.org/toolsforadventure/games/index.html

Level	Title	Author	Genre	Text Type	Themes	Comprehension Strategies	Phonics And Word Study	Writing Options	Technology
Q	Finding the Titanic	Robert D. Ballard	Informational Text	Chapter Book	making discoveries; exploring under the sea; learning about historic events; using graphic aids and captions	Using Captions	Suffixes -er and -est	expository descriptive	http://www.pbs.org/lostliners/titanic.html http://www.rmstitanic.net/index.php?4page=faq
Q	LaRue Across America: Postcards From the Vacation	Mark Teague	Fantasy	Series Book	traveling across America; dealing with disappointment; helping a friend; communicating through writing	Generating Questions	Context Clues	list letter	http://www.historyplace.com/tourism/usa.htm/ http://egsc.usgs.gov/isb/pubs/teach-pack/mapshow/posterandpacket.html
Q	Magic Pickle and the Planet of the Grapes	Scott Morse	Adventure	Series Book	solving crimes; being a superhero; understanding word play; helping others	Making Predictions	Idioms	descriptive narrative	http://www.scholastic.com/magicpickle http://kidsbiology.com/animals-for-children.php
Q	Nothing Ever Happens on 90th Street	Roni Schotter	Realistic Fiction	Picture Book	using your imagination; consequences of stretching the truth	Making Inferences	Synonyms	persuasive narrative	www.kidsnewsroom.org/coolschools/makeastory/makeastory.asp http://pbskids.org/zoom/activities/café
Q	Shrek!	William Steig	Fantasy	Picture Book	the importance of being yourself; finding that beauty is relative; finding your way in the world; seeking a life partner	Understanding Character	Comparative Adjectives	descriptive poetry	http://www.kidsreads.com/features/0522-shrek.asp http://www2.scholastic.com/browse/article.jsp?id=3754284
Q	Stallion in Spooky Hollow (Animal Ark)	Ben M. Baglio	Mystery	Series Book	fearing the unknown; seeing beyond the surface; treatment of animals; keeping secrets	Recognizing Setting	Multiple-Meaning Words	expository descriptive	http://www2.scholastic.com/browse/contributor.jsp?id=3118 http://www.smuggling.co.uk/index.html
Q	The Tale of Anton Brown and Grace Hopper	Caryn Hart	Fractured Fable	Play	learning a lesson; being kind to others; helping others; doing what you love	Identifying Plot	Context Clues	narrative expository	http://www.aesopfables.com http://www.factmonster.com/dk/encyclopedia/olympics.html
R	Clarice Bean Spells Trouble	Lauren Child	Realistic Fiction	Series Book	the importance of role models; finding the good in difficult situations; fitting in; learning and using new words	Understanding Point of View	Context Clues	narrative persuasive	http://www2.scholastic.com/browse/search?query=lauren+%20child http://www.scholastic.com/kids/stacks/games/%20lt%=stacks/nav/games
R	The Dragon of Lonely Island	Rebecca Rupp	Fantasy	Chapter Book	taking a special family vacation; learning from stories; using your abilities to help others; getting along with siblings	Recognizing Main Idea	Synonyms	descriptive diary	http://animal.discovery.com/convergence/dragons/myth/myth.html http://kidshealth.org/kid/feeling/thought/volunteering.html
R	Episode Two: Invasion of the Relatives (Julian Rodriguez)	Alexander Stadler	Fantasy	Graphic Novel	feeling different from those around you; celebrating a holiday with relatives; using imagination; getting along with family	Making Inferences	Prefixes and Suffixes	list descriptive	http://www.scholastic.com/julianrodriguez/author.htm http://www.nickjr.com/recipes/all-shows/seasonal_thanksgiving/all-ages/index.jhtml
R	Freedom Crossing	Margaret Goff Clark	Historical Fiction	Chapter Book	refraining from judgment; helping others in need; learning about the underground railroad; identifying injustice	Understanding Character	Using Vivid Verbs	letter narrative	http://www.teacher.scholastic.com/activities/bhistory/underground_railroad http://www.americaslibrary.gov/aa/tubman/aa_tubman_subj.html
R	Magic Pickle: The Full Color Graphic Novel!	Scott Morse	Fantasy	Graphic Novel	bringing about justice; having self-confidence; understanding word play; helping others	Understanding Text Structure	Onomatopoeia	narrative descriptive	http://www.ala.org/ala/aboutala/offices/publishing/booklinks/resources/its_elementary_graphic_novels.cfm http://pbskids.org/sagwa/color/flipbook/index.html
R	Miracles on Maple Hill	Virginia Sorensen	Realistic Fiction	Chapter Book	the effects of war on people's lives; the dynamics of a family; adapting to change (moving); growing and changing	Understanding Character	Multiple-Meaning Words	descriptive narrative	http://kids.yahoo.com/directory/Around-the-World/U.S.-States/Pennsylvania http://www.massmaple.org
R	Owen & Mzee: The True Story of a Remarkable Friendship	Isabella Hatkoff, Craig Hatkoff, and Dr. Paula Kahumbu	Informational Text	Picture Book	forming bonds; cooperating to help an animal; being friends; learning from animals	Summarizing	Suffixes	narrative review	http://www.owenandmzee.com/omweb/kidsboma.html http://www.readingrockets.org/books/fun/writingcontest/level2
R	Sitting Down for Dr. King	Charles Ryder	Historical Fiction	Play	acknowledging equal rights; understanding features of a play; recalling historical events; having empathy for others	Understanding Cause and Effect	Informal Language	letter expository	http://www.biography.com/blackhistory/featured-biography/martin-luther-king.jsp http://www.historyplace.com/speeches/anthony.htm
R	What to Do About Alice?	Barbara Kerley	Biography	Picture Book	learning about a president's daughter; finding out ways of enjoying life; living in the public eye; traveling around the world	Understanding Character	Figurative Language: Figures of Speech	narrative expository	http://www.theodoreroosevelt.org/life/familytree/AliceLongworth.htm http://blog.usa.gov/roller/govgab/entry/kids_in_the_white_house
R	Who Cracked the Liberty Bell?	Peter and Connie Roop	Informational Text	Chapter Book	fighting for rights and freedom; using revolution to bring about change; learning America's history; reasoning for revolt	Understanding Historical Content	Diphthongs ou, ow	poetry narrative	http://www.theamericanrevolution.org http://www.archives.gov/historical-docs
S	Amelia Earhart: This Broad Ocean	Sarah Stewart Taylor and Ben Towle	Biography/ Historical Fiction	Graphic Novel	finding courage; striving for equality of opportunity; embarking on adventure; using one's skills	Understanding Historical Context	Colloquialisms and Idioms	expository narrative	http://www.americaslibrary.gov/aa/earhart/aa_earhart_subj.html http://www.nytimes.com/learning/general/onthisday/big/0702.html#article
S	Confessions of a Gym-Class Dropout	Chuck Ranberg and Patrick Daley	Realistic Fiction	Play	ways of gaining self-respect; setting and achieving one's goals; bullying; dealing with social politics	Understanding Cause and Effect	Compound Words	persuasive procedural	http://kidshealth.org/kid/stay_healthy/fit/fit_kid.html http://www.ymcastrongkids.org/skhome2.htm
S	The Dinosaurs of Waterhouse Hawkins	Barbara Kerley	Biography	Picture Book	recognizing the importance of knowledge; pursuing a passion; taking a peek at the past; dealing with success and failure	Understanding Main Idea and Details	Context Clues	expository narrative	http://www2.scholastic.com/browse/article.jsp?id=4740 http://en.origami-club.com/easy/dinosaur/index.html
S	From the Mixed-Up Files of Mrs. Basil E. Frankweiler	E. L. Konigsburg	Mystery	Chapter Book	discovering clues; revealing secrets; knowing one's strengths; working as a team	Understanding Point of View	Antonyms	graphic aid expository	http://www.metmuseum.org/explore/publications/pdfs/Kids_Map_LR.pdf http://www.amnh.org/exhibitions/
S	The Good Dog	Avi	Fantasy	Chapter Book	overcoming obstacles; standing up for what you believe in; instincts vs. learned behavior; being part of a group (leadership)	Visualizing	Strong Verbs	expository narrative	http://nationalzoo.si.edu/Animals/NorthAmerica/Facts/fact-graywolf.cfm http://www.pbs.org/wgbh/nova/wolves

Level	Title	Author	Genre	Text Type	Themes	Comprehension Strategies	Phonics And Word Study	Writing Options	Technology
S	The Houdini Box	Brian Selznick	Historical Fiction	Picture Book	meeting someone you idolize; finding out what you see is not always what you get; illusions in magic acts and human interaction; dealing with disappointment	Understanding Plot	Synonyms	poster descriptive	http://www.pbs.org/wgbh/amex/houdini/ http://life.familyeducation.com/writing/writing-composition/49060.html
S	Out of Darkness: The Story of Louis Braille	Russell Freedman	Biography	Chapter Book	overcoming challenges; accepting and creating new ideas; recognizing the accomplishments of others; standing up for what is right	Summarizing	Suffixes -sion and -tion	descriptive narrative	http://www.mathsisfun.com/braille-translation.html http://www.greatideasforkids.com/articles--advice/newsletter-editorials/
S	Taking Sides	Gary Soto	Realistic Fiction	Chapter Book	starting over; finding one's place in the world; being on a team; differences (race)	Comparing and Contrasting	Idioms	descriptive expository	http://kidshealth.org/kid/feeling/home_family/moving.html http://www.usatoday.com/sports/default.htm
S	When Women Played Baseball	Caryn Hart	Historical Fiction	Play	playing baseball; recognizing the impact of World War II; understanding women's history; displaying courage	Understanding Character	Suffix -er	letter expository	http://education.baseballhalloffame.org/experience/thematic_units/womens_history.html http://www.aagpbl.org/articles/interviews.cfm
S	The Young Man and the Sea	Rodman Philbrick	Realistic Fiction	Chapter Book	taking on responsibility; being determined; seeking adventure; discovering personal strength	Recognizing Story Structure	Regional Phrases	list card	http://www.takemefishing.org/fishing/family/fish-with-your-kids http://www.bangordailynews.com/detail/101529.html
T	Colonial Times: 1600-1700	Joy Masoff	Informational Text	Picture Book	adapting in a new place; understanding colonial American history; interacting with unfamiliar cultures; undertaking a difficult journey	Understanding Cause and Effect	Possessives	journal persuasive	http://www.americaslibrary.gov/jb/colonial/jb_colonial_subj.html http://www.histarch.uiuc.edu/plymouth/texts.html
T	The Dodgeball Chronicles (Knights of the Lunch Table)	Frank Cammuso	Fantasy	Graphic Novel	finding help from unexpected sources; discovering weakness in bullies; finding hidden talents; appreciating friends of all kinds	Understanding Cause and Effect	Homonyms	list narrative	http://encyclopedia.kids.net.au/page/ki/King_Arthur http://www.funandgames.org/games/GameDodgeball.htm
T	It Only Looks Easy	Pamela Curtis Swallow	Realistic Fiction	Chapter Book	things are not always as they appear; shedding a bad reputation; dealing with repercussions of actions; empathy	Understanding Theme	Onomatopoeia	descriptive narrative	http://www.quotationspage.com/subjects/reputation http://www.avma.org/animal_health/brochures/veterinarian/veterinarian_brochure.pdf
T	Life in the Oceans: Animals, People, Plants	Lucy Baker	Informational Text	Picture Book	learning about oceans; identifying marine plants and animals; protecting the earth; understanding ecosystems	Identifying Main Idea and Supporting Details	Compound Words	expository narrative	http://www.noaa.gov/ocean.html http://www.lastormwater.org/siteorg/residents/howucnhp.htm
T	Mudshark	Gary Paulsen	Mystery	Chapter Book	solving problems; helping people see things in new ways; appreciating others' talents; leading a team	Making Predictions	Suffix -ion	narrative expository	http://teacher.scholastic.com/writewit/mystery/tips.htm http://pbskids.org/zoom/activities/sci/colorsplash.html
T	Sir Arthur Conan Doyle's The Red-Headed League	Caryn Hart	Mystery	Play	recognizing the importance of details; solving a mystery; understanding features of a play; recognizing clues	Understanding Plays	Recognizing Adverbs	descriptive narrative	http://www.sherlockholmesonline.org/index.htm www.kids.gov/6_8/6_8_careers.shtml
T	Smile	Raina Telgemeier	Memoir	Graphic Novel	understanding true friendship; overcoming life's obstacles; finding humor in adversity; recognizing who we can rely on	Making Inferences	Recognizing Slang	poem graphic aid	http://www.adha.org/kidstuff/faqs.htm http://www.scholastic.com/smile/index.htm
T	Tracker	Gary Paulsen	Realistic Fiction	Chapter Book	coming to terms with loss; interacting with the natural world; understanding the preciousness of life; working at something until it is complete	Understanding Character	Adverbs	poem procedural	http://childgrief.org/howtohelp.htm www.dnr.state.wi.us/org/caer/ce/eek/critter/mammal/fawn.htm
T	The Word Eater	Mary Amato	Fantasy	Chapter Book	seeing the consequences of our actions; every action has a consequence; turning a bad situation into something positive; treating power responsibly	Understanding Plot	Similes	expository narrative	http://kidshealth.org/kid/feeling/friend/clique.html http://www2.scholastic.com/browse/classmags.jsp?srcid=76
T	The Wright 3	Blue Balliett	Mystery	Novel	noticing details; using strengths and talents to solve problems; trusting your friends; protecting one's heritage	Understanding Point of View	Latin Roots	descriptive graphic aid	http://www.franklloydwright.org/fllwf_web_091104/Home.html http://www.philly.com/inquirer/opinion/101053974.html
U	The BFG	Roald Dahl	Fantasy	Novel	making a difference in the world; good versus evil; overcoming evil; being different; doing what's right	Visualizing	Multisyllabic Words	letter list	http://www.roalddahl.com http://www.epa.gov/opptead1/Publications/whyreadlabel.pdf
U	The Calder Game	Blue Balliett	Mystery	Novel	solving a mystery; exploring art; helping a friend; playing a game	Understanding Problem and Solution	Similes and Metaphors	expository narrative	http://whitney.org/Collection/AlexanderCalder http://www.scouting.org.za/codes/sliding.php
U	The Extraordinary Mark Twain (According To Susy)	Barbara Kerley	Biography	Picture Book	exploring the life of Mark Twain; exploring features of a biography; observing important details; describing important events in a life	Understanding Point of View	Difficult Words	narrative expository	http://www.cmgww.com/historic/twain http://shs.umsystem.edu/famousmissourians/writers/clemens/clemens.shtml
U	The Fairy-Tale Detectives (The Sisters Grimm)	Michael Buckley	Fantasy	Series Book	seeing beyond people's appearances; uncovering family history; adapting to change; dealing with a difficult situation	Drawing Conclusions	Synonyms	narrative poetry	http://www.literaturepage.com/read/grimms-fairy-tales.html http://www2.scholastic.com/browse/lessonplan.jsp?id=1177
U	My Side of the Mountain	Jean Craighead George	Realistic Fiction	Novel	searching for adventure; becoming independent; survival in the wild; urban vs. rural	Visualizing	Multiple-Meaning Words	narrative persuasive	http://www.catskillcenter.org http://teacher.scholastic.com/writewit/news/step1.htm
U	Road to Revolution!	Stan Mack and Susan Champlin	Historical Fiction	Graphic Novel	defending your beliefs; understanding the American Revolution; helping a friend in trouble; learning about life in colonial America	Understanding Graphic Novels	Context Clues	narrative graphic aid	http://www.nps.gov/revwar/about_the_revolution/overview.html http://library.thinkquest.org/TQ0312848/quotes.htm
U	The Ruins of Gorlan (Ranger's Apprentice)	John Flanagan	Fantasy	Series Book	finding one's purpose; the effects of bullying; undergoing a process of learning; exploring one's identity	Recognizing Story Structure	Compound Words	descriptive expository	http://www.kidsonthenet.com/castle/view.html http://pbskids.org/wayback/family/tree/tree_tips.html
U	Sir Arthur Conan Doyle's Sherlock Holmes and the Blue Carbuncle	Charles Ryder	Mystery	Play	making observations; uncovering clues to solve a crime; meeting a challenge; understanding human nature	Understanding Character	Synonyms	narrative expository	http://www.mysterynet.com/holmes/ http://www.learner.org/workshops/middlewriting/images/pdf/jw-drama%20class.pdf

Level	Title	Author	Genre	Text Type	Themes	Comprehension Strategies	Phonics And Word Study	Writing Options	Technology
U	The Star Crusher (Missile Mouse)	Jake Parker	Science Fiction	Graphic Novel	fighting crime; taking risks to solve problems; using advanced technology; working as a secret agent	Understanding Flashbacks	Using Context Clues	descriptive narrative	http://library.buffalo.edu/libraries/asl/guides/graphicnovels http://www.factmonster.com/
U	Wringer	Jerry Spinelli	Realistic Fiction	Novel	dealing with peer pressure; standing up for one's beliefs; rationalizing violence; treatment of animals	Understanding Theme	Similes	graphic aid narrative	http://www.hsus.org/wildlife http://www.birds.cornell.edu/pigeonwatch/resources/cool-facts-about-pigeons
V	The Bad Beginning (A Series of Unfortunate Events)	Lemony Snicket	Adventure	Series Book	overcoming adversity; using cleverness to overcome evil; relying on family; taking care of one another	Understanding Characters	Using Synonyms	persuasive expository	http://www.lemonysnicket.com http://www.crayola.com/products/splash/color_explosion/index.cfm?n_id=57
V	Black Star, Bright Dawn	Scott O'Dell	Realistic Fiction	Novel	finding independence; growing up by facing life's challenges; exhibiting bravery even when one feels afraid; admiring one's parent	Visualizing	Understanding Idioms	narrative graphic aid	http://www.iditarod.com http://www.jhuapl.edu/education/elementary/newspapercourse/samplenewspapers/samples.htm
V	The Capture (Guardians of Ga'hoole)	Kathryn Lasky	Fantasy	Series Book	thinking for yourself; believing in yourself; understanding that knowledge is power; recognizing the qualities of a hero	Making Predictions	Context Clues	persuasive narrative	http://www.allaboutbirds.org/NetCommunity/Page.aspx?pid=1189 http://nationalzoo.si.edu/animals
V	The Cats in Krasinski Square	Karen Hesse	Historical Fiction	Free Verse	displaying courage in trying times; helping others; surviving against all odds; working together	Identifying Point of View	Personification	journal expository	http://fcit.usf.edu/HOLOCAUST/timeline/ghettos.htm http://www.bbc.co.uk/history/worldwars/wwtwo/ww2_summary_01.shtml
V	Double-Dare to Be Scared: Another Thirteen Chilling Tales	Robert D. San Souci	Mystery	Short Stories	being afraid of the unknown; separating reality from fantasy; facing fearful situations; relating to the fears of others	Identifying Reality and Fantasy	Similes	descriptive persuasive	http://www.sonomalibrary.org/booklists/KidsScaryStories.html http://www.timeforkids.com
V	Ghostopolis	Doug TenNapel	Fantasy	Graphic Novel	facing your fears; fighting against evil; rebuilding family relationships; having hope	Understanding Setting	Informal Language	descriptive narrative	http://ww2.scholastic.com/content/collateral_resources/pdf/g/Scholastic_GraphixPages01.pdf http://ww2.scholastic.com/browse/book.jsp?id=1313833
V	Heat	Mike Lupica	Realistic Fiction	Novel	desire to immigrate; consequences of dishonesty; following one's dreams in difficult situations; getting support from friends	Understanding Character	Strong Action Verbs	narrative expository	http://www.mikelupicabooks.com http://www.littleleague.org/learn/programs/asap/safetyposters.htm
V	Lewis Carroll's Alice in Wonderland	Play Version by Anne Coulter Martens	Fantasy	Play	growing up; thinking for oneself; distinguishing fantasy from reality; questioning authority	Understanding Dramatic Elements	Homophones	expository narrative	http://www.cs.cmu.edu/~rgs/alice-table.html http://ww2.scholastic.com/browse/article.jsp?id=1178
V	Sojourner Truth: Ain't I a Woman?	Patricia C. McKissack and Fredrick McKissack	Biography	Chapter Book	acting on passionate convictions; dealing with tragedy as well as triumph; valuing oneself; inspiring others	Identifying Fact and Opinion	Reading Difficult Words	expository list	http://rmc.library.cornell.edu/abolitionism/narratives.htm http://www.sojournertruth.org/Library/Speeches/Default.htm
V	The Titanic	Deborah Kent	Informational Text	Picture Book	learning about the Titanic; studying historical documents; learning from mistakes; identifying inequalities	Understanding Cause and Effect	Negative Prefixes	narrative persuasive	http://www.si.edu/encyclopedia_si/nmah/titanic.htm http://library.duke.edu/digitalcollections/adaccess
W	The Great Cow Race (Bone)	Jeff Smith	Fantasy	Graphic Novel	appreciating genuine friends; finding out that scheming often leads to trouble; expecting the unexpected; adjusting when plans fall through	Drawing Conclusions	Reading Homophones	expository narrative	www.scholastic.com/bone/author.htm http://ww2.scholastic.com/browse/article.jsp?id=3750337
W	Houdini: The Handcuff King	Jason Lutes and Nick Bertozzi	Biography/Historical Fiction	Graphic Novel	entertaining others; taking risks for show and reward; reaching a goal; amazing others	Understanding Historical Context	Onomatopoeia	expository descriptive	http://www.scholastic.com/graphix http://www.apl.org/history/houdini/biography.html
W	I Am a Star: Child of the Holocaust	Inge Auerbacher	Autobiography	Chapter Book	triumph in the face of adversity; a person's will to survive; the power of personal perspective; the effects of war	Generating Questions	Prefixes	poetry graphic	http://www.ushmm.org/education/foreducators http://www.ushmm.org/outreach/en
W	Max the Mighty: A Novel	Rodman Philbrick	Realistic Fiction	Novel	building a friendship; being different from others; showing compassion for others; standing up to a bully	Understanding Cause and Effect	Colloquialisms	persuasive narrative	www2.scholastic.com/browse/collateral.jsp?id=858 type=Book_typeId=2779 http://pbskids.org/itsmylife/friends/bullies/index.html
W	Mind Readers: Science Examines ESP	Thomasine E. Lewis Tilden	Informational Text	Chapter Book	debating the existence of ESP; listening to arguments; learning about unexplained phenomena; conducting tests	Understanding Steps in a Process	Context Clues	Procedural narrative	http://ww2.scholastic.com/products/classroombooks/24.7.htm http://www.bls.gov/k12/social04.htm
W	Numbering All the Bones	Ann Rinaldi	Historical Fiction	Novel	overlooking evil; dealing with loss; making choices; choosing freedom	Understanding Character	Similes	expository narrative	http://www.nps.gov/history/seac/andearch.html http://www25.uua.org/uuhs/duub/articles/clarabarton.html
W	The Phantom Tollbooth	Play Version by Susan Nanus	Fantasy	Play	going on an adventure; appreciating words and wordplay; avoiding trivial distractions; learning from mistakes	Understanding Figurative Language	Context Clues	descriptive narrative	http://www.salon.com/books/int/2001/03/12/juster/print.html http://www.wordcentral.com
W	Stowaway	Karen Hesse	Historical Fiction	Novel	life at sea in the 1700s; consequences of using child labor; witnessing difficult events; exploring a historical event through the eyes of a child	Drawing Conclusions	Compound Words	narrative persuasive	http://library.thinkquest.org/J002678F/why.htm http://www.maptools.com/UsingLatLon
W	The Titan's Curse (Percy Jackson & the Olympians)	Rick Riordan	Adventure	Novel	sacrificing to help others; using personal strengths to overcome obstacles; being loyal; finding your place in the world	Understanding Problem and Solution	Multisyllabic Words	persuasive narrative	http://edsitement.neh.gov/view_lesson_plan.asp?id=234 http://tipdeck.com/how-to-draw-a-map
W	Torn Thread	Anne Isaacs	Historical Fiction	Novel	appreciating how precious life is; understanding the effects of extreme prejudice; recognizing the hardships of war; sacrificing for others	Understanding Setting	Understanding Similes	narrative graphic aid	http://ww2.scholastic.com/browse/collateral.jsp?id=1368_type=Book_typeId=3221 http://americanhistory.si.edu/victory/victory2.htm
X	Any Small Goodness: A Novel of the Barrio	Tony Johnston	Realistic Fiction	Novel	relying on family; appreciating one's neighborhood; believing in humanity; living in a city	Monitoring Comprehension	Unfamiliar Words: Using a Glossary	expository narrative	http://www.pbs.org/americanfamily/eastla.html http://pbskids.org/mayaandmiguel/english/print/fajita.html
X	Elijah of Buxton	Christopher Paul Curtis	Historical Fiction	Novel	understanding the power of hope; taking risks to help others; freedom vs. oppression; (not losing) hope	Understanding Point of View	Similes	expository narrative	http://teacher.scholastic.com/activities/bhistory/underground_railroad http://teacher.scholastic.com/LessonPlans/AnswerSheet.pdf

Level	Title	Author	Genre	Text Type	Themes	Comprehension Strategies	Phonics And Word Study	Writing Options	Technology
X	Harlem Summer	Walter Dean Myers	Historical Fiction	Novel	exploring opportunities; discovering one's identity; being shaped by one's surroundings; meeting real historical figures in fiction	Making Predictions	Dialect	expository descriptive	http://www.pbs.org/newshour/forum/february98/harlem_2-20.html http://www.poetryfoundation.org/archive/poet.html?id=3340
X	King George III: America's Enemy	Philip Brooks	Biography	Chapter Book	learning about historical figures; exploring the role of a king; evaluating arguments in persuasive writing; using supplemental resources and graphic aids	Generating Questions	Using Context Clues	graphic aid persuasive	http://www.bbc.co.uk/history/historic_figures/george_iii_king.shtml http://socialstudieged.com/persuade.html
X	The Legend of Hong Kil Dong: The Robin Hood of Korea	Anne Sibley O'Brien	Folktale	Graphic Novel	fighting for justice for others; creating your own destiny; right vs. wrong; dedication	Understanding Problem and Solution	Suffixes -ation and -ion	narrative graphic aid	http://teacher.scholastic.com/writewit/mff/ http://itdc.lbcc.edu/cps/english/phonicSounds/intro.htm
X	The Little Prince	Antoine de Saint Exupéry	Fantasy	Novel	finding friendship; discovering what is important in life; using one's imagination; making difficult decisions	Understanding Theme	Multisyllabic Words	descriptive narrative	http://www.pbs.org/kcet/chasingthesun/innovators/aexupery.html http://science.nasa.gov
X	The Mostly True Adventures of Homer P. Figg	Rodman Philbrick	Historical Fiction	Novel	exaggeration/imagination vs. truth; tragedies of war and slavery; truth vs. falsity; self-presentation	Understanding Character	Metaphors	poetry narrative	http://www.civilwar.org/education/teachers http://cwar.nps.gov/civilwar/abcivwarTimeline.htm
X	O. Henry's The Gift of the Magi	Play Version by Anne Coulter Martens	Realistic Fiction	Play	making a sacrifice for a loved one; appreciating what one has; comparing adaptations; caring about other people	Understanding Plays	Adverbs	narrative expository	http://www.auburn.edu/~vestmon/Gift_of_the_Magi.html http://www.watchessuperstore.com/watchessuperstore-Childrens-Watches-cid-22-list.html
X	Satchel Paige: Striking Out Jim Crow	James Sturm and Rich Tommaso	Biography/Historical Fiction	Graphic Novel	facing and overcoming prejudice; living during the era of segregation; responding with dignity; learning about a famous athlete	Drawing Conclusions	Multiple-Meaning Words	descriptive expository	http://academic.udayton.edu/race/02rights/jcrow02.htm http://blogs.publishersweekly.com/blogs/shelftalker/?p=358
X	Stanford Wong Flunks Big-Time	Lisa Yee	Realistic Fiction	Novel	lying to impress others; accepting yourself as you are; making assumptions about others; feeling inadequate	Comparing and Contrasting	Prefixes in- and un-	graphic aid letter	http://www.multcolib.org/kids/booklists/4-5.html http://topics.nytimes.com/topics/reference/timestopics/subjects/c/childrens_books/index.html
Y	All the Broken Pieces	Ann E. Burg	Historical Fiction	Free Verse	healing after tragedy; learning empathy for others; forgiving ourselves and others; understanding the aftermath of war	Making Inferences	Recognizing Metaphors	expository poem	http://www.pbs.org/wgbh/amex/daughter/peopleevents/e_babylift.html http://www.fns.usda.gov/tn/tnrockyrun/ways.htm
Y	Artemis Fowl: The Graphic Novel	Eoin Colfer and Andrew Donkin	Adventure	Graphic Novel	good versus evil; consequences of overconfidence; feeling the need to salvage one's reputation; continuing family traditions	Understanding Character	Suffixes	narrative descriptive	www2.scholastic.com/browse/collateral.jsp?id=1399 http://www.howstuffworks.com/tunnel.htm
Y	Bad Boy: A Memoir	Walter Dean Myers	Memoir	Chapter Book	understanding family dynamics; being true to oneself; discovering the importance of supportive people in one's life; forming one's own unique identity	Identifying Cause and Effect	Antonyms	letter expository	http://www.walterdeanmyers.net http://teacher.scholastic.com/writewit/poetry/karla_home.htm
Y	Children of the Dust Bowl	Jerry Stanley	Informational Text	Chapter Book	dealing with the environment; class distinctions and prejudice; understanding an important historical time period; people having the power to make a difference	Identifying Cause and Effect	Suffixes	descriptive persuasive	http://www.pbs.org/wgbh/americanexperience/films/dustbowl/player http://www.geosoc.org/schools/adult/english/persuade.html
Y	The Devil's Arithmetic	Jane Yolen	Historical Fiction	Novel	remembering the Holocaust; surviving against all odds; sacrificing for family	Visualizing	Understanding Irony	descriptive narrative	http://www.ushmm.org/wlc/en/article.php?ModuleId=10005143 http://www.marthastewart.com/cooking-with-kids
Y	Jackaroo: A Novel in the Kingdom	Cynthia Voigt	Adventure	Series Book	overcoming limitations imposed by society based on gender and class; using disguises for different reasons; heroism despite adversity; feudalism	Understanding Theme	Similes	narrative expository	http://www.learner.org/interactives/middleages/feudal.html http://www.timeforkids.com/TFK/kids/news/story/0,28277,1937785,00.html
Y	Milkweed	Jerry Spinelli	Historical Fiction	Novel	enduring adversity; finding one's identity at different stages of life; exploring the dynamics of family; life following tragedy	Understanding Point of View	Similes	expository narrative	http://www.ushmm.org/wlc/en/article.php?ModuleId=10005069 www.momentmag.com/moment/issues/2009/06/Jerry_Spinelli.html
Y	Riot	Walter Dean Myers	Historical Fiction	Screenplay	defining one's identity; overcoming the power of prejudice; ignorance and bigotry; class differences	Understanding Historical Context	Idioms	narrative list	http://www.screenwritersfederation.org/writing.asp www.hyperhistory.com/online_n2_History_n2/a.html
Y	Truce	Jim Murphy	Informational Text	Chapter Book	trying to understand why nations go to war; understanding why soldiers might defy leaders and orders; good nature; sentimental values (holidays and family)	Understanding Historical Context	Understand-ing Figurative Language	expository narrative	http://www.bbc.co.uk/history/worldwars/wwone http://www.loc.gov/rr/program/bib/wwi/wwi.html
Y	Weedflower	Cynthia Kadohata	Historical Fiction	Novel	finding friends in unlikely places; facing injustice with strength of character; feeling close to family; experiencing cultural conflict and harmony	Making Inferences	Suffixes	letter persuasive	http://pbskids.org/wayback/fair/fair/fighters/fighters_01_1.html http://www.letterwritingguide.com/friendlyletterformat.htm
Z	Chains	Laurie Halse Anderson	Historical Fiction	Novel	overcoming great obstacles; surviving tragedy; fighting for freedom; understanding different perspectives	Understanding Setting	Understanding Compound Words	list persuasive	http://www.theamericanrevolution.org http://www.earlyamerica.com/earlyamerica/milestones/commonsense
Z	Chasing Lincoln's Killer	James L. Swanson	Informational Text	Chapter Book	recounting the events of history; understanding people's motivation; changing the course of history; facing consequences of actions	Making Inferences	Proper Nouns	expository play	http://www.whitehouse.gov/about/presidents/abrahamlincoln http://www.nytimes.com
Z	Countdown	Deborah Wiles	Historical Fiction	Novel	dealing with fear; exploring a specific time in American history; learning about families and social structures; analyzing documentary	Understanding Plot	Context Clues	expository narrative	http://teachinghistory.org/nhec-blog/23484 http://www.dropcoverholdon.org
Z	The Evolution of Calpurnia Tate	Jacqueline Kelly	Historical Fiction	Novel	finding your identity; exploring the world around you; growing up; learning from one another	Understanding Point of View	Strong Verbs	descriptive graphic aid	http://www.jacquelinekelly.com/ http://www.scholastic.com/magicschoolbus/games/experiments/index.htm
Z	The Glass Menagerie	Tennessee Williams	Realistic Fiction	Play	using hope to deny reality; sacrificing personal freedom for duty; family values and relations; gender roles	Understanding Theme	Using Word Variations	opinion persuasive	http://www.milwaukeerep.com/pdfs/Glass%20SG.pdf http://www2.scholastic.com/browse/lessonplan.jsp?id=64
Z	The Hunger Games	Suzanne Collins	Science Fiction	Series Book	rebelling against an unjust society; making sacrifices; finding traces of true cultural implications in fiction; young people exhibiting bravery	Understanding Character	Multisyllabic Words	narrative persuasive	http://www.publishersweekly.com/pw/print/00000000/42087-children-s-books-apocalypse-now.html http://teacher.scholastic.com/scholasticnews/indepth/index.asp
Z	The Many Rides of Paul Revere	James Cross Giblin	Biography	Chapter Book	exploring the life of a historical figure; fighting for independence; standing up for your rights; making sacrifices	Understanding Cause and Effect	Difficult Words	expository graphic aid	http://www.pbs.org/ktca/liberty http://www.paulreverehouse.org/ride/virtual.shtml

Level	Title	Author	Genre	Text Type	Themes	Comprehension Strategies	Phonics And Word Study	Writing Options	Technology
Z	**Stormbreaker: The Graphic Novel (Alex Rider)**	Anthony Horowitz and Antony Johnston	Adventure	Graphic Novel	facing personal challenges; having courage in the face of danger; learning about your strengths; showing courage	Making Predictions	Reading Multiple-Meaning Words	persuasive narrative	http://www.anthonyhorowitz.com/alexrider http://www2.scholastic.com/browse/article.jsp?id=3751228
Z	**Tales From Outer Suburbia**	Shaun Tan	Fantasy	Short Stories	making sense of the world; finding meaning in fantasy; looking differently at what seems familiar; discerning between reality and fantastical events	Understanding Structure	Multisyllabic Words	description narrative	http://nationalhumanitiescenter.org/tserve/nattrans/ntuseland/essays/citsubs.htm http://library.thinkquest.org/J001156/forms%2Dof%20writing/sl_howto.htm
Z	**Uglies**	Scott Westerfeld	Science Fiction	Series Book	making choices on your own behalf; living in a futuristic world; choosing sides; surviving	Visualizing	Personification	descriptive letter	http://jefferson.lib.co.us/pdf/sififorkids.pdf http://www.scottwesterfeld.com/books/uglies.htm

GUIDED READING RESEARCH BASE

Essential Element	Key Ideas—National Reading Panel
Phonemic Awareness Instruction in Guided Reading • Children use their beginning connections between letters and sounds to check on their reading. They notice mismatches. They use letter-sound information to know how words begin. • Teachers prompt children to make their reading "look right."	"Phonemic awareness instruction is not a complete reading program; it cannot guarantee the reading and writing success of your students. Long lasting effects depend on the effectiveness of the whole curriculum." (3, p. 9) "Phonemic awareness instruction does not need to consume long periods of time to be effective. In these analyses, programs lasting less than 20 hours were more effective than longer programs." (2, p. 2–6) "In addition to teaching phonemic awareness skills with letters, it is important for teachers to help children make the connection between the skills taught and their application to reading and writing tasks." (2, p. 2–33)
Phonics Instruction in Guided Reading • Teachers select texts that, along with high-frequency words that are available to students, offer opportunities to use phonics skills. • As they introduce texts, support reading, and revisit the text after reading, teachers bring students' attention to features of words and strategies for decoding words. • Students apply word solving strategies to reading continuous texts. • Teachers explicitly demonstrate how to take words apart and apply phonics principles to new words students meet in continuous text. • Teachers explicitly teach phonics principles through word work after the text is read. Word work sessions are connected to a phonics continuum. • Teachers prompt students to use phonics skills to take words apart while reading.	"Children need opportunities to use what they have learned in problem solving unfamiliar words that they encounter within continuous text. They use word solving strategies to take words apart while keeping the meaning in mind." (3, p. 18) "Reading words accurately and automatically enables children to focus on the meaning of text." (3) "Programs should acknowledge that systematic phonics instruction is a means to an end. Some phonics programs focus primarily on teaching children a large number of letter-sound relationships. These programs often do not allot enough instructional time to help children learn how to put this knowledge to use in reading actual words, sentences, and texts. Although children need to be taught the major consonant and vowel letter-sound relationships, they also need ample reading and writing activities that allow them to practice this knowledge." (3, p. 17)
Fluency Instruction in Guided Reading • Texts are selected to be within students' control so that they know most of the words and can read fluently (with teaching). • The teacher introduces the text to support comprehension and connections to language. • Teachers draw students' attention to elements of words that will help them recognize or solve them rapidly.	"If text is read in a laborious and inefficient manner, it will be difficult for the child to remember what has been read and to relate the ideas expressed in the text to his or her background knowledge." (1, p. 22) "Repeated and monitored oral reading improves reading fluency and overall reading achievement." (3, p. 11) "It is important to provide students with instruction and practice in fluency as they read connected text." (3, p. 23) "Word recognition is a necessary but not sufficient condition for fluent reading." (3, p. 30) "Fluency is not a stage of development at which readers can read all words quickly and easily. Fluency changes, depending on what readers are reading, their familiarity with the words, and the amount of their practice with reading text." (3, p. 23)

• Teachers help students to understand and use the language patterns that may be found in written text. • Students use word recognition and comprehending strategies in an orchestrated way while reading or rereading a text silently or orally. • Teachers provide explicit demonstrations and instruction in reading fluency. • Teachers prompt for fluency when students are reading aloud. • Students engage in repeated oral readings to work for fluency.	"By listening to good models of fluent reading, students learn how a reader's voice can help written text make sense." (3, p. 26) "Fluency develops as a result of many opportunities to practice reading with a high degree of success. Therefore, your students should practice orally rereading text that is reasonably easy for them—that is, text containing mostly words that they know or can decode easily." (3, p. 27)
Vocabulary Instruction in Guided Reading • Texts are selected so that students know most of the words but there are a few new words to provide opportunities for learning. • The teacher introduces the text to support comprehension, with specific attention to concepts and words. • Students read the text silently or orally with teacher support. • After reading, students and teacher discuss the meaning of the text, with further discussion of word meanings if needed. • The teacher teaches processing strategies, which may include both word recognition and how to determine word meanings. • Students may extend the meaning of the text through writing, which often includes attention to vocabulary. • The teacher provides 1–2 minutes of pre-planned word work which helps students attend to word parts and word meanings (affixes, word structure, homophones, synonyms, etc.).	"Extended instruction that promotes active engagement with vocabulary improves word learning." (3, p. 36) "Teaching specific words before reading helps both vocabulary learning and reading comprehension." (3, p. 36) "Repeated exposure to vocabulary in many contexts aids word learning." (3, p. 36) "Conversations about books help children to learn new words and concepts and to relate them to their prior knowledge and experience." (3, p. 35) "… the larger the reader's vocabulary (either oral or print), the easier it is to make sense of the text." (1, p. 13) "… children often hear adults repeat words several times. They also may hear adults use new and interesting words. The more oral language experiences children have, the more word meanings they learn." (3, p. 35)
Comprehension Instruction in Guided Reading • Teachers select texts that readers can process successfully with supportive teaching. • The teacher demonstrates effective strategies for comprehending text. • In the introduction to the text, the teacher explains words and concepts and assures that students activate their own prior knowledge. • Students have the opportunity to apply a range of strategies in response to the demands of texts.	"Comprehension is defined as 'intentional thinking during which meaning is constructed through interactions between text and reader' (Harris & Hodges, 1995). Thus, readers derive meaning from text when they engage in intentional, problem-solving thinking processes. The data suggest that text comprehension is enhanced when readers actively relate the ideas represented in print to their own knowledge and experiences and construct mental representations in memory." (1, p. 14) "In general, the evidence suggests that teaching a combination of reading comprehension techniques is the most effective. When students use them appropriately, they assist in recall, question answering, question generation, and summarization of texts. When used in combination, these techniques can improve results in standardized comprehension tests." (1, p. 15) "Text comprehension can be improved by instruction that helps readers use specific comprehension strategies." (2, p. 49)

• Students expand strategies by applying them, with teacher support, to texts that are more difficult than they could read independently. • Teachers help students extend their understandings through using oral language and writing. • Teachers help students extend their understanding through using graphic organizers to understand underlying text structures. • While teachers are working with students in small groups, other students read independently the books that they have previously read.	"Text comprehension can be improved by instruction that helps readers use specific comprehension strategies." (3, p. 9) "Graphic organizers illustrate concepts and interrelationships among concepts in a text, using diagrams or other pictorial devices. Regardless of the label, graphic organizers can help readers focus on concepts and how they are related to other concepts." "Comprehension strategies are not ends in themselves; they are means of helping your students understand what they are reading." (3, p. 6) "Help your students learn to use comprehension strategies in natural learning situations—for example, as they read in the content areas." (3, p. 65) "Readers must know what most of the words mean before they can understand what they are reading." (3, p. 45) "Children learn many new words by reading extensively on their own. The more children read on their own, the more words they encounter and the more word meanings they learn." (3, p. 35) "Teachers not only must have a firm grasp of the content presented in text, but also must have substantial knowledge of the strategies themselves, of which strategies are most effective for different students and types of content and of how best to teach and model strategy use." (1, p. 16)
Motivation Support in Guided Reading • Teachers select books that will be interesting to students. • Teachers introduce texts in a way that engages interest and motivation.	"Few if any studies have investigated the contribution of motivation to the effectiveness of phonics programs, not only the learner's motivation to learn but also the teacher's motivation to teach. The lack of attention to motivational factors by researchers in the design of phonics programs is potentially very serious … Future research should … be designed to determine which approaches teachers prefer to use and are most likely to use effectively in their classroom instruction." (2)
Motivation Support in Guided Reading • Teachers select books that will be interesting to students. • Teachers introduce texts in a way that engages interest and motivation.	"Interesting texts also provide mutual cognitive and motivational benefits (Schiefele, 1999). When students are interested in what they read, they process the material more deeply, gain richer conceptual understandings, and engage more fully with text." (4, p. 416)
Motivation Related to Reading Comprehension • Students who receive motivation support and strategy instruction improve their reading comprehension.	"Motivated students usually want to understand text content fully, and therefore, process information deeply. As they read frequently with these cognitive purposes, motivated students gain in reading proficiency. However, motivation and engagement have rarely been incorporated into experimental studies of instruction or interventions for reading comprehension." (4, p. 403) "(a) Engagement in reading refers to interaction with text that is simultaneously motivated and strategic, (b) engaged reading correlates with achievement in reading comprehension, (c) engaged reading and its constituents (motivation and cognitive strategies) can be increased by instruction practices directed toward them, and (d) an instructional framework that merges motivational and cognitive strategy support in reading will increase engaged reading and reading comprehension." (4, p. 403)

Effect of Engagement on Interest in Reading • Motivated readers are able to monitor their comprehension, recall what they read, and retain and organize the knowledge they gain. • Motivated readers are involved in their reading, often rereading and reflecting on their understanding. • Motivated readers know how reading is relevant to their lives. • Engaged readers find that reading is a meaningful, enjoyable activity.	"...the most highly interested students had positive affect toward books, favored certain authors, and enjoyed favorite topics. These high interest readers typically reread all or portions of books, pursued topics in and out of school, and connected reading to their personal experiences or feelings. Also salient was the students' deep comprehension and complex cognitive command of these texts that accompanied their enjoyment and enthusiasm. Students with high positive affect for a certain topic invariably had deep recollection of information or books about the topic, whereas students with low affect for reading on a topic displayed little recall and grasp of content. This suggests that high interest in reading is not limited to the strong, positive affect surrounding books, but also the high comprehension, recall, and organization of knowledge in memory typical of these readers." (5, p. 13)
Readers' Motivation to Be Responsible for Their Own Learning • Engaged readers are in control of their own learning and are able to express their opinions and their own understandings.	"A substantial proportion of students reported that knowledge and information was what they were seeking in books. We did not create this as a formal construct nor place it in our rubric, because we did not systematically ask all students about the extent that they read for knowledge. However, many students volunteered that they wanted to learn about their favorite topic, enjoyed gaining information, or liked being very well informed in certain domains. Being knowledgeable was an explicit goal mentioned by many, and while it is a commonsense purpose for reading, it has not been formalized quantitatively in prior research as a motivational construct. We believe that reading for the purpose of knowledge development is a vitally important motivational attribute for future investigation." (5, p. 26)
Readers' Engagement With Text • For engaged readers, reading is a highly visual experience as they imagine characters, settings, and events. • Readers who are emotionally engaged in text can often note and understand ideas the author does not explicitly state. • Readers engage in an interchange of ideas between themselves and the text.	"...reading narrative text is often affectively laden, and that readers adopt affective goals for narrative reading. They seek excitement, emotional relationship with characters, interpersonal drama, and a range of aesthetic experiences. Reading information books, in contrast, is energized by goals of reading for knowledge, seeking information, and the desire to explain our physical or cultural worlds. Thus, motivations for reading narrative and information books should be distinguished in studying how motivation develops or how it relates to other factors such as reading comprehension." (5, p. 26-27)
Features of Engaging Classrooms • Engaging classrooms are observational, conceptual, self-directed, strategic, collaborative, coherent, and personalized.	"To increase motivational development, teachers should provide support for situated experiences that increase intrinsic motivation. For example, an exciting activity that may be entertaining, such as reader's theater for a specific book, may increase situated, intrinsic motivation. Likewise, hands-on activities with science materials (a terrarium with plants and animals, or a field trip to a park) or hands-on activities in history (a reenactment of a historical scene within the classroom) will increase situated, intrinsic motivation for texts related to these topics. However, these events will be insufficient to influence long-term motivation for reading. Experimental evidence suggests that increasing generalized intrinsic motivation requires the extended classroom practices of support for students' choices, collaborations, use of interesting texts, and real-world interactions related to literacy." (6, p. 21)

The ideas in this chart are referenced to the following documents:

(1) National Institute of Child Health and Human Development. (2001). *Report of the National Reading Panel: Teaching Children to Read: An Evidence-Based Assessment of the Scientific Research Literature on Reading and Its Implications for Reading Instruction.* Washington, DC: National Institutes of Health.

(2) National Institute of Child Health and Human Development. (2001). *Report of the National Reading Panel: Teaching Children to Read: An Evidence-Based Assessment of the Scientific Research Literature on Reading and Its Implications for Reading Instruction: Report of the Subgroups.* Washington, DC: National Institutes of Health.

(3) Armbruster, B. B., Lehr, F., & Osborn, J. (2001). *Put Reading First: The Research Building Blocks for Teaching Children to Read, Kindergarten through Grade 3.* Washington, DC: U.S. Department of Education.

[i] "Readers must know what most of the words mean before they can understand what they are reading." (*Put Reading First,* p. 45)

[ii] "Beginning readers use their oral vocabulary to make sense of the words they see in print ... Readers must know what most of the words mean before they can understand what they are reading." (*Put Reading First,* p. 45)

(4) Guthrie, John T.; Wigfield, Allan; Barbosa, Pedro, et al., "Increasing Reading Comprehension and Engagement Through Concept-Oriented Reading Instruction," *Journal of Education Psychology,* 2004, Vol. 96, No 3, 403–423.

(5) Guthrie, John T.; Hoa, Laurel W.; Wigfield, Allan; Tonks, Stephen M.; Humneick, Nicole M.; Littles, Erin, "Reading Motivation and Reading Comprehension Growth in the Later Elementary Years," *Contemporary Educational Psychology,* June 3, 2006.

(6) Guthrie, John T.; Hoa, Laurel W.; Wigfield, Allan; Tonks, Stephen M.; Perencevich, Kathleen C., "From Spark to Fire: Can Situational Reading Interest Lead to Long Term Reading Motivation?" *Reading Research and Instruction,* v45, n2, pp. 91–117, Winter 2006, College Reading Association, Brigham Young University, Provo, UT.

BIBLIOGRAPHY

Allington, R. L. (2009). *What really matters in response to intervention.* New York: Addison-Wesley Longman.

Anderson, E., and Guthrie, J. T. (1999). *Motivating children to gain conceptual knowledge from text: The combination of science observation and interesting texts.* Paper presented at the annual meeting of the American Educational Research Association, Montreal, Canada.

Atwell, N. (2008). *The reading zone: How to help kids become skilled, passionate, habitual, critical readers.* New York: Scholastic.

Biancarosa, G., Bryk, A., & Dexter, E. (2009). Assessing the value-added effects of coaching on student learning. Final report to the Institute of Education Sciences (IES).

Blevins, Wiley, and Boynton, Alice. "5 Keys to Reading Nonfiction." *The Art of Teaching.* Supplement to *Instructor Magazine:* 4–7.

Bolter, J. D. (2001). *Writing space: Computers, hypertext, and the remediation of print.* Mahwah, NJ: Lawrence Erlbaum Associates.

Box, J., et al. (2009). *The mile guide: Milestones for improving learning & education.* Tucson, AZ: The Partnership for 21st Century Skills.

Braunger, J., and Lewis, J. (2008). "What we know about the learning and development of reading K-12: Thirteen core understandings about reading and learning to read." *What research really says about teaching and learning to read.* Edited by S. Kucer. Urbana, IL: NCTE.

Brown, H., and Cambourne, B. (1987). *Read and retell: A strategy for the whole-language/natural learning classroom.* Portsmouth, NH: Heinemann.

Burke, Jim. (2000). *Reading reminders: Tools, tips, and techniques.* Portsmouth, NH: Heinemann

Chall, J. S. (1983). *Stages of reading development.* New York: McGraw-Hill.

Clay, M. M. (1993). *Reading Recovery: A Guidebook for Teachers in Training.* Portsmouth, NH: Heinemann.

Common core state standards for English language arts & literacy in history/social studies, science, and technical subjects (2010). Washington, DC: Common Core Standards Initiative.

Cortese, A., & Ravitch, D. (2008). Preface in *Still at risk What students don't know, even now.* Washington, DC: Common Core.

Darling-Hammond, L. (2010). *The flat world and education: How America's commitment to equity will determine our future.* New York: Teacher's College Press.

Dreher, M. J. (2000). Fostering reading for learning. In L. Baker, M. J. Dreher & J. Guthrie (Eds.), *Engaging young readers: Promoting achievement and motivation* (pp. 94–118). New York: Guilford.

Duke, Nell K., and Bennett-Armistead, V. Susan (2003). *Reading & Writing Informational Text in the Primary Grades: Research-Based Practices.* New York, NY: Scholastic Inc.

Dymock, S. (2005). Teaching expository text structure awareness. *The Reading Teacher,* 59(2), 177–181.

Essential components of RTI – A closer look at response to intervention. (2010). Washington, DC: National Center on Response to Intervention. Retrieved from: http://www.rti4success.org/index.php?option=com_content&task=view&id=448&Itemid=93

Fountas, I., & Pinnell, G. S. (2006). *Teaching for comprehending and fluency: Thinking, talking, and writing about reading, K-8.* Portsmouth, NH: Heinemann, p. 429.

Fountas, I. & Pinnell, G. S. (2009). *When readers struggle: Teaching that works.* Portsmouth, NH: Heinemann.

Fountas, Irene, and Pinnell, G. S. (1996). *Guided Reading: Good First Teaching for All Children*. Portsmouth, NH: Heinemann.

Fountas, Irene, and Pinnell, G. S. (2001). *Guiding Readers and Writers, Grades 3–6*. Portsmouth, NH: Heinemann.

Fountas, Irene, and Pinnell, G. S., eds. (1999). *Voices on Word Matters*. Portsmouth, NH: Heinemann.

Gibson, Akimi, Gold, Judith, and Sgouras, Charissa. (2003). "The Power of Story Retelling." *The Tutor*. Spring 2003.

Hoffman, J. V., Roser, N. L., Salas, R., Patterson, E., & Pennington, J. (2000). *Text leveling and little books in first-grade reading* (CIERA Report No. 1-0). Ann Arbor: Center for the Improvement of Early Reading Achievement, University of Michigan.

Jobe, R., & Dayton-Sakari, M. (2002). *Info-kids: How to use nonfiction to turn reluctant readers into enthusiastic learners*. Markham, Ontario, Canada: Pembroke.

Johnston, P. (In Press). Response to Intervention in Literacy: Problems and Possibilities. *Elementary School Journal*.

Kamil, M. L., & Lane, D. M. (1998). Researching the relation between technology and literacy: An agenda for the 21st century. In D. R. Reinking, L. D. Labbo, M. McKenna, & R. Kieffer (Eds.), *Literacy for the 21st century: Technological transformations in a post-typographic world* (pp. 235–251). Mahwah, NJ: Erlbaum.

Pinnell, Gay Su, and Fountas, I. C. (1999). *Matching Books to Readers: A Leveled Book List for Guided Reading, K–3*. Portsmouth, NH: Heinemann.

Pinnell, Gay Su, and Fountas, I. C. (1998). *Word Matters: Teaching Phonics and Spelling in the Reading/Writing Classroom*. Portsmouth, NH: Heinemann.

Pinnell, G. S., Pikulski, J. J., Wixson, K. K., Campbell, J. R., Gough, R. B., and Beatty, A. S. (1995). *Listening to Children Read Aloud: Data from NAEP's Integrated Reading Performance Record (IPRR) at Grade 4*. Report No. 23-FR-04 Prepared by Educational Testing Service under contract with the National Center for Education Statistics, Office of Educational Research and Improvement, U.S. Department of Education. (p. 15)

Reading framework for the 2009 National Assessment of Educational Progress. (2009). National Assessment Governing Board. Washington, DC. Retrieved from: http://www.nagb.org/publications/frameworks/reading09.pdf

Resnick, L. (1987). The 1987 Presidential address: Learning in school and out: Educational Researcher. December 1987. vol. 16. no. 9. pp. 13–54

Taylor, B. M., Pearson, P. D., Clark, K., & Walpole, S. (2000). Effective schools and accomplished teachers: Lessons about primary grade reading instruction in low income schools. *Elementary School Journal*, 101, 121–165.

Trilling, B. & Fadel, C. (2009). *21st Century Skills: Learning for Life in Our Times*. San Francisco, CA: Jossey-Bass.

Venezky, R. L. (1982). The origins of the present-day chasm between adult literacy needs and school literacy instruction. *Visible Language, 16,* 112–127.

RESEARCH AND VALIDATION

A strong pattern of rising scores has been found in schools where daily guided reading has been combined with phonics and word study mini-lessons and daily writing workshops. For further information, see:

Williams, Jane. (2002). The power of data utilization in bringing about systemic school change. *Mid-Western Educational Researcher,* 15, 4–10.

Williams, E. J., Scharer, P., & Pinnell, G. S. (2000). *Literacy Collaborative 2002 Research Report.* Columbus, OH: The Ohio State University.

Scharer, P., Williams, E. J., & Pinnell, G. S. (2001). *Literacy Collaborative 2001 Research Report.* Columbus, OH: The Ohio State University.